## THE ORIGIN OF GROUP ANALYSIS

In speaking of social or group psychology it has become usual . . . to isolate as the subject of inquiry the influencing of an individual by a large number of people simultaneously. . . .

Group psychology is therefore concerned with the individual man as a member of a race, of a nation, of a caste, of a profession, of an institution, or as a component part of a crowd of people. . . .

It is easy to regard the phenomena that appear under these special conditions as being expressions of a special instinct that is not further reducible—the social instinct. . . .

Our expectation [however] is directed toward two other possibilities: that the social instinct may not be a primitive one and insusceptible of dissection, and that it may be possible to discover the beginnings of its development in a narrower circle, such as that of the family. . . .

From the Introduction by
**Sigmund Freud**

BANTAM MATRIX EDITIONS

# group psychology and the analysis of the ego

•

by Sigmund Freud

•

Translated by James Strachey

With an Introduction
by Franz Alexander

BANTAM BOOKS
NEW YORK/TORONTO/LONDON

GROUP PSYCHOLOGY AND THE ANALYSIS OF THE EGO
A Bantam Book / published by arrangement with
Liveright Publishing Corp.

Bantam Classic edition published April 1960
2nd printing ...... May 1960
3rd printing ... October 1961
4th printing .. February 1963
5th printing ... January 1964
Bantam Matrix edition published July 1965

7th printing
8th printing

Bantam Books are published by Bantam Books, Inc., a subsidiary
of Grosset & Dunlap, Inc. Its trade-mark, consisting of the words
"Bantam Books" and the portrayal of a bantam, is registered in the
United States Patent Office and in other countries. Marca Registrada.
Bantam Books, Inc., 271 Madison Avenue, New York, N. Y. 10016.

# CONTENTS

INTRODUCTION, by Franz Alexander....... vii

EDITOR'S NOTE ......................... 1

I. INTRODUCTION ....................... 3
II. LE BON'S DESCRIPTION OF THE GROUP MIND 6
III. OTHER ACCOUNTS OF COLLECTIVE MENTAL
LIFE ................................. 19
IV. SUGGESTION AND LIBIDO................. 26
V. TWO ARTIFICIAL GROUPS: THE CHURCH AND
THE ARMY ......................... 32
VI. FURTHER PROBLEMS AND LINES OF WORK... 40
VII. IDENTIFICATION ...................... 46
VIII. BEING IN LOVE AND HYPNOSIS........... 54
IX. THE HERD INSTINCT.................... 62
X. THE GROUP AND THE PRIMAL HORDE...... 69
XI. A DIFFERENTIATING GRADE IN THE EGO..... 78
XII. POSTSCRIPT .......................... 85

BIBLIOGRAPHY ......................... 99

INDEX ................................103

# INTRODUCTION

For over thirty years, Freud refrained from building a comprehensive system from his arduously collected observations made during the treatment of his patients. Thus, he was an outstanding representative of the Hippocratic tradition of bedside medicine: his conclusions came from innumerable detailed observations made on individual patients. He was the first among modern psychologists to interest himself in man as an individual person—not in general terms, but in Mr. Smith as a unique case whose emotional problems must be understood on the basis of his own specific life history. Freud used the empirical inductive method to its full in a field in which hitherto speculation and deductive reasoning had reigned for centuries.

Freud repeatedly protested against being considered a philosopher. He conceived psychoanalysis as a scientific discipline: the first methodical study of the human personality, previously the exclusive domain of creative writers. In all his writings, he meticulously distinguished between observation and speculation; even in his speculative writings he started out from what he considered basic, incontestable facts.

Only at the end of the last century when all psychologists still held university chairs of philosophy, did psychology begin to emancipate itself from philosophy. Earlier time physics, chemistry and biology had ceased to be called Natural Philosophy, and the social sciences escaped the designation of Social Philosophy. Freud, a medical psychologist, felt the need to state his position emphatically: he considered himself first of all a scientist who builds his theoretical concepts on detailed studies of individual persons.

*Group Psychology and the Analysis of the Ego* belongs to that group of Freud's systematic writings in which this modern Hippocrates of medical psychology makes an attempt to integrate his observations and more or less fragmented concepts into a comprehensive view of the human mind. The first book in this group, *Beyond the Pleasure Principle* (1920), appeared a year before *Group Psychology* and was followed two years later by *The Ego and the Id* (1922)—the culmination of his system-building efforts.

While *Beyond the Pleasure Principle* is an attempt to revise and systematize his earlier concepts about instincts, *Group Psychology* and *The Ego and the Id* concern themselves with the structure of the personality—of the Ego. They were preceded by a more fragmented attempt, his article on "narcissism." In these three books, Freud, the physician, is no longer concerned with mental pathology, but uses all that he learned from the painstaking study of mentally disturbed patients for drawing an admittedly first rough draft of the construction and functioning of the normal mind. In this volume much of what he formulated three years later in *The Ego and the Id* appears in a more rudimentary form. It conveys the atmosphere of the workroom. Freud takes up many subjects only to leave them unfinished as brilliant but provisional formulations; these include the origin of social justice as a reaction against siblings' rivalry, the problem of identification, the similarities between being in love and hypnosis. He also returns to his widely criticized theory of the primal horde of brothers ruled by a tyrannical, powerful father, which he considered as the beginning of human society—a concept first advanced by Charles Darwin. After the rebellious sons killed the chief, the horde changed into a fraternal society—a community of brothers. The deep-seated longing of the brothers for a powerful leader, however, reasserted itself and led to totemism and later to religious systems —the totem and the deity being the reincarnation of the murdered father. Freud is thoroughly impressed by the indestructibility of the profound emotional need of humanity for strong leadership, which is the cornerstone of all his sociological speculations. It reveals his dim view about the viability of democracies— a view which could be supported by the fact that the human race succeeded in establishing free democratic social systems only for two short periods during its known history: once in Athens and then again in modern Western civilization. In between these two rare occurrences, humanity always lived under the dictatorship of feudal or centralized rulers. Biologists may also adduce the evidence that living organisms consisting of individual cells, have always—with rare exceptions, such as sponges—a "head end" which coordinates and rules over the activities of the constituent parts.

The concept of the Superego—the internalized precipitate of parental guidance which Freud elaborated a few years later in *The Ego and the Id*—is closely related to this basic orientation. The Superego is foreshadowed by the less clearly defined, vaguer concept of the Ego Ideal, used synonymously with "conscience." Freud's Superego definitely has the characteristics of an absolute, primarily punitive ruler as it actually reveals itself in such psychopathological conditions as the depressions and obsessional-compulsive neuroses. In mature persons, however, it can be no longer sharply differentiated from the Ego, which governs by principles more like those prevailing in democratic societies: judgment, flexibility and compromise.

In *Group Psychology* Freud gives full recognition to

Le Bon's deservedly famous work, *Psychologie Des Foules* (1895). Le Bon's main thesis is that, as a part of a group, man regresses to a primitive mental state. Isolated he may be a cultivated individual; in the group he is capable of acting as a barbarian, is prone to violence, loses his critical faculties, becomes emotional and may lose all his moral standards and inhibitions. His critical, intellectual ability and control yield to emotionalism, suggestibility and inconsistency. He becomes unpredictable, inconsistent, similar to primitive man or to a child. In groups the individual features of a person, his superstructure, disappears, yielding to the homogeneous common substratum which is preserved as an ancestral heritage in man's unconscious. At the same time new features appear: as a member of a larger group, man feels more powerful while his individual responsibility diminishes since he shares it with all other members of the group.

Freud agrees with this description of Le Bon, but explains the regressive features of mob psychology by his own formulation concerning the nature of human conscience. The essence of conscience is "social anxiety," the fear of public opinion. In following the herd, social anxiety necessarily disappears in the members of the group. As Le Bon, Freud also calls the primitive attitudes which appear in the members of a group "unconscious" trends; but Freud points out that Le Bon's "unconscious" is not identical with his. For Le Bon, these deeply buried features of the mind constitute the archaic heritage of man. Le Bon is not aware of that part of the unconscious mind which, because it is unacceptable to the conscience, is *repressed*. The power behind repression is the conscience. The dynamic concept of repression was not known to Le Bon. In the group, the voice of the individual conscience is silenced. Hence, all that has been repressed, all that violates the standards of the conscience, can now uninhibitedly appear in behavior.

Freud also follows Le Bon in comparing the behavior of the members of the group to that of persons in the state of hypnosis. Freud, however, raises the question: Who is the hypnotizer? Le Bon pays little attention to the leader of the group. For Freud, the leader is the key figure in group psychology. It is he who subjects the members to his hypnotic spell.

Neither Le Bon nor McDougall—another author who influenced Freud in his group-psychological speculations—penetrated to the essence of the problem: What are the forces which hold groups together? What are the psychological factors which make a group a group, rather than a number of individuals gathered in a bunch? No matter how brilliant Le Bon's observations are, they remain brilliant descriptions which, however, fail to explain the central features of group behavior: heightened suggestibility, ebbing of intellectual-critical faculties, and the "mental contagion" by which group members mutually enhance their common emotions. "Mental contagion," which Le Bon uses for explanation, is but an analogy, a figure of speech which, itself, requires further explanation.

Freud contends that the key figure in every organized or loosely organized, randomly assembled group is the leader. The group member's relationship to the leader explains also the relations of the members to each other. The leader becomes the individual member's common ego ideal and takes over all the critical faculties, just as the hypnotized individual abandons his self-determination for the sake of the hypnotizer. This common bond which ties every member of the group to the leader also determines their inter-relationship. By their common attachment to the leader, they can identify themselves with each other.

To explain the nature of the group member's attachment to the leader, Freud borrows his most fundamental concept, that of *libido*, precisely "aim inhibited libido" or desexualized libido. This is the cohesive, unifying force which binds individual units into higher entities, higher organizations. While the members are bound by libidinous ties to their leader, the leader's psychology sharply differs from that of the members. He has no emotional attachments to anybody but himself and it is precisely this narcissistic quality which makes him a leader. "He loves no one but himself, or other people insofar as they can serve his needs." He is "of masterly nature," "self-confident" and "independent." He represents all those qualities which the group members themselves cannot attain. Thus he becomes their Ego Ideal.

By introducing the concept of libido which ties the members of the group to the leader, Freud can dispense with Trotter's "herd instinct" as the force responsible for group cohesion. Freud's explanation is unquestionably more elegant since he operates with a concept which was successful in explaining the mutual relationships between the members of what is undoubtedly the most elementary social group—the family. The mutual attachments between the members of the family reveal themselves as libidinous ties, and do not require the invention of a special new kind of instinct. The same principle can be thus applied to account for bonds within the family as well as for those operative in the larger extension of the family: in social groups.

The contemporary reader will miss in Freud's theory a more precise definition of the emotional ties of the group members to the leader. He will find the concept of libido too general. From the vantage point of modern psychoanalytical theory, this emotional relationship can be more precisely described as a return to the infant's dependent attitude toward his parents. There are plenty of references in Freud's text to the dependent nature of this tie, but he does not make full use of its significance. The regressive nature of group behavior finds satisfactory explanation if one stresses the childlike dependence of the members upon their leader. Under the spell of the leader, the group members renounce the internalized parental image (their own conscience) and relegate its role to the leader. They regress to a phase in their development in which they were blindly following the voice and guidance of their parents. During the process of emotional maturation, the child gradually adopts the standards and values of the parents by *identifying* himself with them. Through this process of identification, he becomes more independent. He no longer needs parental guidance after he firmly internalizes their guiding principles into his own personality. He now carries the parental standards inside of himself and no longer needs the actual parents for guidance. Becoming the member of a group, he relegates to the leader the functions of the parents and thus the whole process of emotional maturation is reversed. Under the spell of a strong leader, the group member becomes a dependent child. Apparently most persons retain sufficient residues of childhood's dependency needs and insecurity to be susceptible to such emotional regression. The blissful security of the Garden of Eden remains an ever-powerful motif in history. Man seems prone to exchange readily the insecurity and struggle of freedom for the security promised by strong leaders. The image of the welfare state is a modern manifestation of the same regressive trend.

The dependence on the leader resolves the apparent contradiction that a group which may become ferocious and destructive is also capable of self-sacrifice and devotion. The outcome obviously depends upon the nature and ideals of the leader who can influence his followers in either direction.

Further, the phenomenon of panic can be more clearly understood by stressing the dependent quality of the members' attachment to their leader. Exposed to a danger, the need for dependence increases; but if faith in the leader is shaken, the members of the group become overwhelmed by paralyzing anxiety. They have given up self-government and replaced it by obedience and faith in the leader. When the leader fails, they are left without any guidance—internal or external: they become like helpless children deserted by their parents.

In war and national emergencies even democratic societies are apt to sacrifice some of their jealously guarded freedoms and confer greater control on their government.

Freud's group psychology has all the earmarks of a pioneering venture. He made only the first tentative steps toward understanding the principles of social organization. Most of his psychological descriptions are applicable only to the phenomena of mob psychology. He was clearly aware of this and tried to apply the same basic principles to the understanding of the emotional structure of firmly organized groups. Selecting the Catholic Church and the Army as examples, he had to account for a contradiction: conscience develops under the influence of parental leadership, yet leadership may be the source of asocial behavior as seen in loosely organized groups. In other words, living in a social group makes man moral and yet, becoming the member of a group led by a strong leader, man may lose his morality. What then are the conditions under which the conscience, itself the precipitate of social standards, may dwindle away through group influences? Freud clearly recognized that the Superego itself originates in social organization inasmuch as the values transmitted by the parents to the child are precisely those which prevail in society.

The Church and the Army were obviously unfortunate choices to formulate the general principles of group dynamics. Freud selected two organizations in which central authority is paramount. The members of both of these organizations retain much of that abject dependence on and obedience to leadership which is characteristic of the child. The central figure is a fatherlike image, and the soldier as well as the flock retain much of childhood's dependency. In this one respect a random group under the spell of a strong leader resembles a structured group organized around a strong authority.

This is not the case in free, democratic societies which consist of more independent, self-governing individuals. Here the attitude toward leadership is quite different. Citizens may trust their leaders, yet they are critically watching them. They elect their leaders and retain the right to vote them out if they do not fulfill their expectations. And the leaders, to a high degree, depend upon their electors. In such societies, the members and the leader are interdependent. Their relation is not as asymmetric as in autocratic systems.

One may justly conclude that Freud's theory of the group was strongly influenced by the social milieu in which he grew up. This may be the reason that he so clearly recognized the role of the leader; yet the very same factors may have induced him to overrate this role. Le Bon and McDougall were oblivious of the significance of the leader. Freud on the other hand was inclined to generalize its role for all forms of social organization. It is true that he occasionally—mostly in parenthesis—refers to the fact that in some societies the leader may be represented not by a human being but by an abstract ideal. He does not, however, elaborate the structure of societies which are held together more by common abstract principles and ideals—such as freedom, individual responsibility and self-government—rather than by a strong leader. Certainly the influence of abstract ideals upon human beings can scarcely be compared with hypnosis. The exalted figure of a leader may, indeed, exert a hypnotic spell upon his followers. But the guiding principles of free societies, the stress on the individual's critical faculty and self-responsibility are contradictory to that blind obedience to authority which is the essence of hypnosis.

Authoritarian organizations, like the Church and the Army, are not suited to throw light upon the regressive phenomena which Le Bon and Freud considered as characteristic of mob psychology. Authoritarian societies, like loosely organized groups which come under the influence of a leader, are based on regressive principles, on childish uncritical obedience. However, only the psychological phenomena which take place in a mob aroused by a leader can truly be called regressive because the persons who constitute the mob otherwise belong to a society in which their individual consciences are effective. Outside of the mob they have higher standards, individual responsibility and critical judgment. The members of hierarchical organizations on the other hand, like the Church and the Army, do not regress but are always dependent on their leaders.

The mentality of free societies can not be explained either by mob psychology or by the spirit prevailing in authoritarian societies.

In spite of the shortcomings of this pioneering venture into the psychodynamics of society, Freud's contribution is of fundamental nature. Some contemporary psychoanalytic authors—often called neo-Freudians—Sullivan, Horney, Thompson, Fromm to mention only a few—came into the habit of attributing to Freud a lack of awareness of cultural factors in the shaping of human personality. They favorably compare Sullivan's "dynamic cultural point of view" with Freud's "mechanistic biological orientation" (Clara Thompson). The thoughtful reader of this volume can easily convince himself of the fallaciousness of this judgment.

Freud was fully aware of the fact that the development of human personality can be understood only if one considers the influences of the prevailing social standards and values to which it is subjected. This is clearly borne out by his terse statement in this book, that "we must conclude that the psychology of the group is the oldest human psychology." Freud considered conscience (Ego Ideal and later Superego) as the precipitate of parental influences which transmit to the child the standards and values of the society in which he matures. Social scientists and psychologists who like to consider themselves distinguished by their cultural orientation, in contrast to Freud's antiquated "19th century biological orientation," actually did not add any new principle to this basic insight. It is true that Freud did not undertake comparative studies on personality development in different cultures. Such studies had to wait until psychoanalytic thought had deeply penetrated into the social sciences and particularly into social anthropology. However, the basic psychological principles by which society exerts its molding influence upon personality development had been laid down by Freud.

FRANZ ALEXANDER

Emeritus Clinical Professor of Psychiatry
University of Southern California
and of
University of Illinois
College of Medicine

# EDITOR'S NOTE

## MASSENPSYCHOLOGIE UND ICH-ANALYSE

*(a)* GERMAN EDITIONS:

1921    Leipzig, Vienna and Zurich: Internationaler
         Psychoanalytischer Verlag. Pp. iii + 140.
1923    2nd ed. Same publishers. Pp. iv + 120.
1925    *G.S.*, 6, 261–349.
1931    *Theoretische Schriften,* 248–337.
1940    *G.W.,* 13, 71–161.

*(b)* ENGLISH TRANSLATION:

*Group Psychology and the Analysis of the Ego*

1922    London and Vienna: International Psycho-
         Analytical Press. Pp. viii + 134. (Tr. J.
         Strachey.)
1940    London: Hogarth Press and Institute of Psycho-
         Analysis; New York: Liveright. (Re-issue of
         above.)

In the first German edition some of the paragraphs
in the text were printed in small type. The English
translator was instructed by Freud at the time to trans-
fer these paragraphs to footnotes. The same transpo-
sition was carried out in all the later German editions
except in the case mentioned on page 35 below. Freud
made some slight changes and additions in the later

editions of the work. The present translation is a considerably altered version of the one published in 1922.

Freud's letters showed that the first "simple idea" of an explanation of group psychology occurred to him during the spring of 1919. Nothing came of this at the time, but in February, 1920, he was working at the subject and he had written a first draft in August of the same year. It was not until February, 1921, however, that he began giving it its final form. The book was finished before the end of March, 1921, and published some three or four months later.

There is little direct connection between the present work and its close predecessor, *Beyond the Pleasure Principle* (1920). The trains of thought which Freud here takes up are more especially derived from the fourth essay in *Totem and Taboo* (1912–13) and his papers on narcissism (1914) (the last paragraph of which raises in a highly condensed form many of the points discussed in the present work) and "Mourning and Melancholia" (1917). Freud also returns here to his early interest in hypnotism and suggestion, which dated from his studies with Charcot in 1885–6.

As is indicated by its title, the work is important in two different directions. On the one hand it explains the psychology of groups on the basis of changes in the psychology of the individual mind. And on the other hand it carries a stage further Freud's investigation of the anatomical structure of the mind which was already foreshadowed in *Beyond the Pleasure Principle* (1920) and was to be more completely worked out in *The Ego and the Id* (1923).

Extracts from the earlier (1922) translation of this work were included in Rickman's *General Selection from the Works of Sigmund Freud* (1937, 195–244).

# GROUP PSYCHOLOGY AND THE ANALYSIS OF THE EGO

## I

## INTRODUCTION

THE contrast between individual psychology and social or group[1] psychology, which at a first glance may seem to be full of significance, loses a great deal of its sharpness when it is examined more closely. It is true that individual psychology is concerned with the individual man and explores the paths by which he seeks to find satisfaction for his instinctual impulses; but only rarely and under certain exceptional conditions is individual psychology in a position to disregard the relations of this individual to others. In the individual's mental life someone else is invariably involved, as a model, as an object, as a helper, as an opponent; and so from the very first individual psychology, in this extended but entirely justifiable sense of the words, is at the same time social psychology as well.

The relations of an individual to his parents and to his brothers and sisters, to the object of his love, and to his physician—in fact all the relations which have hitherto been the chief subject of psychoanalytic re-

[1] ["Group" is used throughout the translation of this work as equivalent to the rather more comprehensive German "*Masse*." The author uses this latter word to render both McDougall's "group," and also Le Bon's "*foule*," which would more naturally be translated "crowd" in English. For the sake of uniformity, however, "group" has been preferred in this case as well, and has been substituted for "crowd" even in the extracts from the English translation of Le Bon.]

3

search—may claim to be considered as social phenomena; and in this respect they may be contrasted
with certain other processes, described by us as "narcissistic," in which the satisfaction of the instincts is
partially or totally withdrawn from the influence of
other people. The contrast between social and narcissistic—Bleuler [1912] would perhaps call them "autistic"—mental acts therefore falls wholly within the
domain of individual psychology, and is not well calculated to differentiate it from a social or group psychology.

The individual in the relations which have already
been mentioned—to his parents and to his brothers
and sisters, to the person he is in love with, to his
friend, and to his physician—comes under the influence of only a single person, or of a very small number
of persons, each one of whom has become enormously
important to him. Now in speaking of social or group
psychology it has become usual to leave these relations
on one side and to isolate as the subject of inquiry the
influencing of an individual by a large number of
people simultaneously, people with whom he is connected by something, though otherwise they may in
many respects be strangers to him. Group psychology
is therefore concerned with the individual man as a
member of a race, of a nation, of a caste, of a profession, of an institution, or as a component part of a
crowd of people who have been organized into a group
at some particular time for some definite purpose.
When once natural continuity has been severed in this
way, if a breach is thus made between things which
are by nature interconnected, it is easy to regard the
phenomena that appear under these special conditions
as being expressions of a special instinct that is not
further reducible—the social instinct ("herd instinct,"
"group mind"),[1] which does not come to light in any
other situations. But we may perhaps venture to object

[1] [These terms are in English in the original.]

that it seems difficult to attribute to the factor of
number a significance so great as to make it capable
by itself of arousing in our mental life a new instinct
that is otherwise not brought into play. Our expectation is therefore directed toward two other possibilities: that the social instinct may not be a primitive
one and insusceptible of dissection, and that it may be
possible to discover the beginnings of its development
in a narrower circle, such as that of the family.

Although group psychology is only in its infancy,
it embraces an immense number of separate issues and
offers to investigators countless problems which have
hitherto not even been properly distinguished from
one another. The mere classification of the different
forms of group formation and the description of the
mental phenomena produced by them require a great
expenditure of observation and exposition, and have
already given rise to a copious literature. Anyone who
compares the narrow dimensions of this little book
with the wide extent of group psychology will at once
be able to guess that only a few points chosen from the
whole material are to be dealt with here. And they will
in fact only be a few questions with which the depth-
psychology of psychoanalysis is specially concerned.

*[handwritten annotations:]*

Group Psychology —

① A component part of an organized
     Crowd — Institution

  a) capable of dissection
  b) development in family relationships

## LE BON'S DESCRIPTION OF THE
## GROUP MIND

INSTEAD of starting from a definition, it seems more useful to begin with some indication of the range of the phenomena under review, and to select from among them a few specially striking and characteristic facts to which our inquiry can be attached. We can achieve both of these aims by means of quotation from Le Bon's deservedly famous work *Psychologie des foules* [1895].

Let us make the matter clear once again. If a psychology, concerned with exploring the predispositions, the instinctual impulses, the motives and the aims of an individual man down to his actions and his relations with those who are nearest to him, had completely achieved its task, and had cleared up the whole of these matters with their interconnections, it would then suddenly find itself confronted by a new task which would lie before it unachieved. It would be obliged to explain the surprising fact that under a certain condition this individual, whom it had come to understand, thought, felt and acted in quite a different way from what would have been expected. And this condition is his insertion into a collection of people which has acquired the characteristic of a "psychological group." What, then, is a "group"? How does it acquire the capacity for exercising such a decisive influence over the mental life of the individual? And what is the nature of the mental change which it forces upon the individual?

6

It is the task of a theoretical group psychology to answer these three questions. The best way of approaching them is evidently to start with the third. Observation of the changes in the individual's reactions is what provides group psychology with its material; for every attempt at an explanation must be preceded by a description of the thing that is to be explained.

I will now let Le Bon speak for himself. He says: "The most striking peculiarity presented by a psychological group[1] is the following. Whoever be the individuals that compose it, however like or unlike be their mode of life, their occupations, their character, or their intelligence, the fact that they have been transformed into a group puts them in possession of a sort of collective mind which makes them feel, think, and act in a manner quite different from that in which each individual of them would feel, think, and act were he in a state of isolation. There are certain ideas and feelings which do not come into being, or do not transform themselves into acts except in the case of individuals forming a group. The psychological group is a provisional being formed of heterogeneous elements, which for a moment are combined, exactly as the cells which constitute a living body form by their reunion a new being which displays characteristics very different from those possessed by each of the cells singly." (Trans. 1920, 29.)

We shall take the liberty of interrupting Le Bon's exposition with glosses of our own, and shall accordingly insert an observation at this point. If the individuals in the group are combined into a unity, there must surely be something to unite them, and this bond might be precisely the thing that is characteristic of a group. But Le Bon does not answer this question; he goes on to consider the alteration which the individual

[1] [See footnote p. 3.—This and the following quotations are from the English translation.]

undergoes when in a group and describes it in terms which harmonize well with the fundamental postulates of our own depth-psychology.

"It is easy to prove how much the individual forming part of a group differs from the isolated individual, but it is less easy to discover the causes of this difference.

"To obtain at any rate a glimpse of them it is necessary in the first place to call to mind the truth established by modern psychology, that unconscious phenomena play an altogether preponderating part not only in organic life, but also in the operations of the intelligence. The conscious life of the mind is of small importance in comparison with its unconscious life. The most subtle analyst, the most acute observer, is scarcely successful in discovering more than a very small number of the conscious[1] motives that determine his conduct. Our conscious acts are the outcome of an unconscious substratum created in the mind mainly by hereditary influences. This substratum consists of the innumerable common characteristics handed down from generation to generation, which constitute the genius of a race. Behind the avowed causes of our acts there undoubtedly lie secret causes that we do not avow, but behind these secret causes there are many others more secret still, of which we ourselves are ignorant.[2] The greater part of our daily actions are the result of hidden motives which escape our observation." (Ibid., 30.)

Le Bon thinks that the particular acquirements of individuals become obliterated in a group, and that in this way their distinctiveness vanishes. The racial unconscious emerges; what is heterogeneous is sub-

[1] [As was pointed out in a footnote in the German edition of 1940, the original French text reads *"inconscients."* The English translation of Le Bon has "unconscious," but the German version, quoted by Freud, has *"bewusster"* ("conscious").]

[2] [The English translation reads "which we ourselves ignore" —a misunderstanding of the French word *"ignorées."*]

merged in what is homogeneous. As we should say, the mental superstructure, the development of which in individuals shows such dissimilarities, is removed, and the unconscious foundations, which are similar in everyone, stand exposed to view.

In this way individuals in a group would come to show an average character. But Le Bon believes that they also display new characteristics which they have not previously possessed, and he seeks the reason for this in three different factors.

"The first is that the individual forming part of a group acquires, solely from numerical considerations, a sentiment of invincible power which allows him to yield to instincts which, had he been alone, he would perforce have kept under restraint. He will be less disposed to check himself, from the consideration that, a group being anonymous and in consequence irresponsible, the sentiment of responsibility which always controls individuals disappears entirely." (Ibid., 33.)

From our point of view we need not attribute so much importance to the appearance of new characteristics. For us it would be enough to say that in a group the individual is brought under conditions which allow him to throw off the repressions of his unconscious instinctual impulses. The apparently new characteristics which he then displays are in fact the manifestations of this unconscious, in which all that is evil in the human mind is contained as a predisposition. We can find no difficulty in understanding the disappearance of conscience or of a sense of responsibility in these circumstances. It has long been our contention that "social anxiety" is the essence of what is called conscience.[1]

[1] There is some difference between Le Bon's view and ours owing to his concept of the unconscious not quite coinciding with the one adopted by psychoanalysis. Le Bon's unconscious more especially contains the most deeply buried features of the racial mind, which as a matter of fact lies outside the scope of psychoanalysis. We do not fail to recognize, indeed, that the

"The second cause, which is contagion, also intervenes to determine the manifestation in groups of their special characteristics, and at the same time the trend they are to take. Contagion is a phenomenon of which it is easy to establish the presence, but which is not easy to explain. It must be classed among those phenomena of a hypnotic order, which we shall shortly study. In a group every sentiment and act is contagious, and contagious to such a degree that an individual readily sacrifices his personal interest to the collective interest. This is an aptitude very contrary to his nature, and of which a man is scarcely capable, except when he makes part of a group." (Ibid., 33.)

We shall later on base an important conjecture upon this last statement.

"A third cause, and by far the most important, determines in the individuals of a group special characteristics which are quite contrary at times to those presented by the isolated individual. I allude to that suggestibility of which, moreover, the contagion mentioned above is only an effect.

"To understand this phenomenon it is necessary to bear in mind certain recent physiological discoveries. We know today that by various processes an individual may be brought into such a condition that, having entirely lost his conscious personality, he obeys all the suggestions of the operator who has deprived him of it, and commits acts in utter contradiction with his character and habits. The most careful investigations seem to prove that an individual immersed for some length of time in a group in action soon finds himself —either in consequence of the magnetic influence given out by the group, or from some other cause of

---

ego's nucleus, which comprises the "archaic heritage" of the human mind, is unconscious; but in addition to this we distinguish the "unconscious repressed," which arose from a portion of that heritage. This concept of the repressed is not to be found in Le Bon.

which we are ignorant—in a special state, which much resembles the state of 'fascination' in which the hypnotized individual finds himself in the hands of the hypnotizer. . . . The conscious personality has entirely vanished; will and discernment are lost. All feelings and thoughts are bent in the direction determined by the hypnotizer.

"Such also is approximately the state of the individual forming part of a psychological group. He is no longer conscious of his acts. In his case, as in the case of the hypnotized subject, at the same time that certain faculties are destroyed, others may be brought to a high degree of exaltation. Under the influence of a suggestion, he will undertake the accomplishment of certain acts with irresistible impetuosity. This impetuosity is the more irresistible in the case of groups than in that of the hypnotized subject, from the fact that, the suggestion being the same for all the individuals in the group, it gains in strength by reciprocity." (Ibid., 34.)

"We see, then, that the disappearance of the conscious personality, the predominance of the unconscious personality, the turning by means of suggestion and contagion of feelings and ideas in an identical direction, the tendency to immediately transform the suggested ideas into acts; these, we see, are the principal characteristics of the individual forming part of a group. He is no longer himself, but has become an automaton who has ceased to be guided by his will." (Ibid., 35.)

I have quoted this passage so fully in order to make it quite clear that Le Bon explains the condition of an individual in a group as being actually hypnotic, and does not merely make a comparison between the two states. We have no intention of raising any objection at this point, but wish only to emphasize the fact that the two last causes of an individual becoming altered in a group (the contagion and the heightened

suggestibility) are evidently not on a par, since the
contagion seems actually to be a manifestation of the
suggestibility. Moreover the effects of the two factors
do not seem to be sharply differentiated in the text of
Le Bon's remarks. We may perhaps best interpret his
statement if we connect the contagion with the effects
of the individual members of the group on one another, while we point to another source for those
manifestations of suggestion in the group which he
regards as similar to the phenomena of hypnotic influence. But to what source? We cannot avoid being
struck with a sense of deficiency when we notice that
one of the chief elements of the comparison, namely
the person who is to replace the hypnotist in the case
of the group, is not mentioned in Le Bon's exposition.
But he nevertheless distinguishes between this influence of "fascination" which remains plunged in obscurity and the contagious effect which the individuals
exercise upon one another and by which the original
suggestion is strengthened.

Here is yet another important consideration for
helping us to understand the individual in a group:
"Moreover, by the mere fact that he forms part of an
organized group, a man descends several rungs in the
ladder of civilization. Isolated, he may be a cultivated
individual; in a crowd, he is a barbarian—that is, a
creature acting by instinct. He possesses the spon-
taneity, the violence, the ferocity, and also the enthusiasm and heroism of primitive beings." (Ibid., 36.) Le
Bon then dwells especially upon the lowering in intellectual ability which an individual experiences when
he becomes merged in a group.[1]

[1] Compare Schiller's couplet:

Jeder, sieht man ihn einzeln, ist leidlich klug und verständig;
  Sind sie in corpore, gleich wird euch ein Dummkopf daraus.
[Everyone, looked at alone, is passably shrewd and discerning;
  When they're *in corpore*, then straightway you'll find he's an
  ass.]

Let us now leave the individual, and turn to the group mind, as it has been outlined by Le Bon. It shows not a single feature which a psychoanalyst would find any difficulty in placing or in deriving from its source. Le Bon himself shows us the way by pointing to its similarity with the mental life of primitive people and of children (ibid., 40).

A group is impulsive, changeable and irritable. It is led almost exclusively by the unconscious.[1] The impulses which a group obeys may according to circumstances be generous or cruel, heroic or cowardly, but they are always so imperious that no personal interest, not even that of self-preservation, can make itself felt (ibid., 41). Nothing about it is premeditated. Though it may desire things passionately, yet this is never so for long, for it is incapable of perseverance. It cannot tolerate any delay between its desire and the fulfillment of what it desires. It has a sense of omnipotence; the notion of impossibility disappears for the individual in a group.[2]

A group is extraordinarily credulous and open to influence, it has no critical faculty, and the improbable does not exist for it. It thinks in images, which call one another up by association (just as they arise with individuals in states of free imagination), and whose agreement with reality is never checked by any reasonable agency. The feelings of a group are always very simple and very exaggerated. So that a group knows neither doubt nor uncertainty.[3]

---

[1] "Unconscious" is used here correctly by Le Bon in the descriptive sense, where it does not mean only the "repressed."

[2] Compare the third essay in my *Totem and Taboo* (1912–13) [*Standard Ed.*, 13, 85 ff.].

[3] In the interpretation of dreams, to which, indeed, we owe our best knowledge of unconscious mental life, we follow a technical rule of disregarding doubt and uncertainty in the narrative of the dream, and of treating every element of the manifest dream as being quite certain. We attribute doubt and uncertainty to the influence of the censorship to which the dream-

It goes directly to extremes; if a suspicion is expressed, it is instantly changed into an incontrovertible certainty; a trace of antipathy is turned into furious hatred (ibid., 56).[1]

Inclined as it itself is to all extremes, a group can only be excited by an excessive stimulus. Anyone who wishes to produce an effect upon it needs no logical adjustment in his arguments; he must paint in the most forcible colors, he must exaggerate, and he must repeat the same thing again and again.

Since a group is in no doubt as to what constitutes truth or error, and is conscious, moreover, of its own great strength, it is as intolerant as it is obedient to authority. It respects force and can only be slightly influenced by kindness, which it regards merely as a form of weakness. What it demands of its heroes is strength, or even violence. It wants to be ruled and oppressed and to fear its masters. Fundamentally it is entirely conservative, and it has a deep aversion to all innovations and advances and an unbounded respect for tradition (ibid., 62).

In order to make a correct judgment upon the

---

work is subjected, and we assume that the primary dream-thoughts are not acquainted with doubt and uncertainty as critical processes. They may of course be present, like anything else, as part of the content of the day's residues which lead to the dream. (See The Interpretation of Dreams (1900), Standard Ed., 5, 516–7.)

[1] The same extreme and unmeasured intensification of every emotion is also a feature of the affective life of children, and it is present as well in dream life. Thanks to the isolation of the single emotions in the unconscious, a slight annoyance during the day will express itself in a dream as a wish for the offending person's death, or a breath of temptation may give the impetus to the portrayal in the dream of a criminal action. Hanns Sachs has made an appropriate remark on this point: "If we look in our consciousness at something that has been told us by a dream about a contemporary (real) situation, we ought not to be surprised to find that the monster which we saw under the magnifying glass of analysis turns out to be a tiny infusorian." (The Interpretation of Dreams (1900), Standard Ed., 5, 620.)

morals of groups, one must take into consideration the
fact that when individuals come together in a group
all their individual inhibitions fall away and all the
cruel, brutal and destructive instincts, which lie dor-
mant in individuals as relics of a primitive epoch, are
stirred up to find free gratification. But under the
influence of suggestion groups are also capable of high
achievements in the shape of abnegation, unselfishness,
and devotion to an ideal. While with isolated individuals personal interest is almost the only motive
force, with groups it is very rarely prominent. It is
possible to speak of an individual having his moral
standards raised by a group (ibid., 65). Whereas the
intellectual capacity of a group is always far below
that of an individual, its ethical conduct may rise as
high above his as it may sink deep below it.

Some other features in Le Bon's description show in
a clear light how well justified is the identification of
the group mind with the mind of primitive people. In
groups the most contradictory ideas can exist side by
side and tolerate each other, without any conflict aris-
ing from the logical contradictions between them. But
this is also the case in the unconscious mental life of
individuals, of children and of neurotics, as psychoanalysis has long pointed out.[1]

---

[1] In young children, for instance, ambivalent emotional attitudes toward those who are nearest to them exist side by side
for a long time, without either of them interfering with the
expression of the other and opposite one. If eventually a conflict
breaks out between the two, it is often settled by the child
making a change of object and displacing one of the ambivalent
emotions on to a substitute. The history of the development of
a neurosis in an adult will also show that a surpressed emotion
may frequently persist for a long time in unconscious or even
in conscious fantasies, the content of which naturally runs
directly counter to some predominant tendency, and yet that
this opposition does not result in any proceedings on the part
of the ego against what it has repudiated. The fantasy is
tolerated for quite a long time, until suddenly one day, usually
as a result of an increase in the affective cathexis of the fan-

A group, further, is subject to the truly magical power of words; they can evoke the most formidable tempests in the group mind, and are also capable of stilling them (ibid., 117). "Reason and arguments are incapable of combating certain words and formulas. They are uttered with solemnity in the presence of groups, and as soon as they have been pronounced an expression of respect is visible on every countenance, and all heads are bowed. By many they are considered as natural forces or as supernatural powers." (Ibid., 117.) It is only necessary in this connection to remember the taboo upon names among primitive people and the magical powers which they ascribe to names and words.[1]

And, finally, groups have never thirsted after truth. They demand illusions, and cannot do without them. They constantly give what is unreal precedence over what is real; they are almost as strongly influenced by what is untrue as by what is true. They have an evident tendency not to distinguish between the two (ibid., 77).

We have pointed out that this predominance of the life of fantasy and of the illusion born of an unfulfilled wish is the ruling factor in the psychology of

---

tasy, a conflict breaks out between it and the ego with all the usual consequences. In the process of a child's development into a mature adult there is a more and more extensive integration of his personality, a co-ordination of the separate instinctual impulses and purposive trends which have grown up in him independently of one another. The analogous process in the domain of sexual life has long been known to us as the co-ordination of all the sexual instincts into a definitive genital organization. (*Three Essays on the Theory of Sexuality*, 1905 [*Standard Ed.*, 7, 207].) Moreover, that the unification of the ego is liable to the same interferences as that of the libido is shown by numerous familiar instances, such as that of men of science who have preserved their faith in the Bible, and other similar cases.—[*Added* 1923:] The various possible ways in which the ego can later disintegrate form a special chapter in psychopathology.

[1] See *Totem and Taboo* (1912–13), *Standard Ed.*, 13, 54–7.

neuroses. We have found that what neurotics are guided by is not ordinary objective reality but psychological reality. A hysterical symptom is based upon fantasy instead of upon the repetition of real experience, and the sense of guilt in an obsessional neurosis is based upon the fact of an evil intention which was never carried out. Indeed, just as in dreams and in hypnosis, in the mental operations of a group the function for testing the reality of things falls into the background in comparison with the strength of wishful impulses with their affective cathexis.

What Le Bon says on the subject of leaders of groups is less exhaustive, and does not enable us to make out an underlying principle so clearly. He thinks that as soon as living beings are gathered together in certain numbers, no matter whether they are a herd of animals or a collection of human beings, they place themselves instinctively under the authority of a chief (ibid., 134). A group is an obedient herd, which could never live without a master. It has such a thirst for obedience that it submits instinctively to anyone who appoints himself its master.

Although in this way the needs of a group carry it half-way to meet the leader, yet he too must fit in with it in his personal qualities. He must himself be held in fascination by a strong faith (in an idea) in order to awaken the group's faith; he must possess a strong and imposing will, which the group, which has no will of its own, can accept from him. Le Bon then discusses the different kinds of leaders, and the means by which they work upon the group. On the whole he believes that the leaders make themselves felt by means of the ideas in which they themselves are fanatical believers.

Moreover, he ascribes both to the ideas and to the leaders a mysterious and irresistible power, which he calls "prestige." Prestige is a sort of domination exercised over us by an individual, a work or an idea. It entirely paralyses our critical faculty, and fills us with wonderment and respect. It would seem to arouse a feeling like that of "fascination" in hypnosis (ibid., 148). He distinguishes between acquired or artificial and personal prestige. The former is attached to persons in virtue of their name, fortune and reputation, and to opinions, works of art, etc., in virtue of tradition. Since in every case it harks back to the past, it cannot be of much help to us in understanding this puzzling influence. Personal prestige is attached to a few people, who become leaders by means of it, and it has the effect of making everyone obey them as though by the operation of some magnetic magic. All prestige, however, is also dependent upon success, and is lost in the event of failure (ibid., 159).

Le Bon does not give the impression of having succeeded in bringing the function of the leader and the importance of prestige completely into harmony with his brilliantly executed picture of the group mind.

## III

# OTHER ACCOUNTS OF COLLECTIVE
# MENTAL LIFE

We have made use of Le Bon's description by way of
introduction, because it fits in so well with our own
psychology in the emphasis which it lays upon unconscious mental life. But we must now add that as a
matter of fact none of that author's statements bring
forward anything new. Everything that he says to the
detriment and depreciation of the manifestations of
the group mind had already been said by others before
him with equal distinctness and equal hostility, and
has been repeated in unison by thinkers, statesmen and
writers since the earliest periods of literature.[1] The two
theses which comprise the most important of Le Bon's
opinions, those touching upon the collective inhibition of intellectual functioning and the heightening
of affectivity in groups, had been formulated shortly
before by Sighele.[2] At bottom, all that is left over as
being peculiar to Le Bon are the two notions of the
unconscious and of the comparison with the mental
life of primitive people, and even these had naturally
often been alluded to before him.

But, what is more, the description and estimate of
the group mind as they have been given by Le Bon
and the rest have not by any means been left undis-
puted. There is no doubt that all the phenomena of
the group mind which have just been mentioned have

---

[1] See Kraškovič (1915), particularly the bibliography.
[2] See Moede (1915).

been correctly observed, but it is also possible to distinguish other manifestations of group formation, which operate in a precisely opposite sense, and from which a much higher opinion of the group mind must necessarily follow.

Le Bon himself was prepared to admit that in certain circumstances the morals of a group can be higher than those of the individuals that compose it, and that only collectivities are capable of a high degree of unselfishness and devotion. "While with isolated individuals personal interest is almost the only motive force, with groups it is very rarely prominent." (Le Bon, trans. 1920, 65.) Other writers adduce the fact that it is only society which prescribes any ethical standards at all for the individual, while he as a rule fails in one way or another to come up to its high demands. Or they point out that in exceptional circumstances there may arise in communities the phenomenon of enthusiasm, which has made the most splendid group achievements possible.

As regards intellectual work it remains a fact, indeed, that great decisions in the realm of thought and momentous discoveries and solutions of problems are only possible to an individual working in solitude. But even the group mind is capable of creative genius in the field of intelligence, as is shown above all by language itself, as well as by folk-song, folklore and the like. It remains an open question, moreover, how much the individual thinker or writer owes to the stimulation of the group in which he lives, and whether he does more than perfect a mental work in which the others have had a simultaneous share.

In face of these completely contradictory accounts, it looks as though the work of group psychology were bound to come to an ineffectual end. But it is easy to find a more hopeful escape from the dilemma. A number of very different structures have probably been merged under the term "group" and may require to be distinguished. The assertions of Sighele, Le Bon and the rest relate to groups of a short-lived character, which some passing interest has hastily agglomerated out of various sorts of individuals. The characteristics of revolutionary groups, and especially those of the great French Revolution, have unmistakably influenced their descriptions. The opposite opinions owe their origin to the consideration of those stable groups or associations in which mankind pass their lives, and which are embodied in the institutions of society. Groups of the first kind stand in the same sort of relation to those of the second as a high but choppy sea to a ground swell.

McDougall, in his book on *The Group Mind* (1920), starts out from the same contradiction that has just been mentioned, and finds a solution for it in the factor of organization. In the simplest case, he says, the "group" possesses no organization at all or one scarcely deserving the name. He describes a group of this kind as a "crowd." But he admits that a crowd of human beings can hardly come together without possessing at all events the rudiments of an organization, and that precisely in these simple groups some fundamental facts of collective psychology can be observed with special ease (McDougall, 1920, 22). Before the members of a random crowd of people can constitute something like a group in the psychological sense, a condition has to be fulfilled: these individuals must have something in common with one another, a common interest in an object, a similar emotional bias in some situation or other, and ("consequently," I should like to interpolate) "some degree of reciprocal influence" (ibid., 23). The higher the degree of "this mental homogeneity," the more readily do the individuals form a psychological group, and the more striking are the manifestations of a group mind.

The most remarkable and also the most important result of the formation of a group is the "exaltation or intensification of emotion" produced in every member of it (ibid., 24). In McDougall's opinion men's emotions are stirred in a group to a pitch that they seldom or never attain under other conditions; and it is a pleasurable experience for those who are concerned, to surrender themselves so unreservedly to their passions and thus to become merged in the group and to lose the sense of the limits of their individuality. The manner in which individuals are thus carried away by a common impulse is explained by McDougall by means of what he calls the "principle of direct induction of emotion by way of the primitive sympathetic response" (ibid., 25), that is, by means of the emotional contagion with which we are already familiar. The fact is that the perception of the signs of an affective state is calculated automatically to arouse the same affect in the person who perceives them. The greater the number of people in whom the same affect can be simultaneously observed, the stronger does this automatic compulsion grow. The individual loses his power of criticism, and lets himself slip into the same affect. But in so doing he increases the excitement of the other people, who had produced this result in him, and thus the affective charge of the individuals becomes intensified by mutual interaction. Something is unmistakably at work in the nature of a compulsion to do the same as the others, to remain in harmony with the many. The cruder and simpler emotional impulses are the more apt to spread through a group in this way (ibid., 39).

This mechanism for the intensification of affect is favored by some other influences which emanate from groups. A group impresses the individual as being an unlimited power and an insurmountable peril. For the moment it replaces the whole of human society, which is the wielder of authority, whose punishments the individual fears, and for whose sake he has submitted to so many inhibitions. It is clearly perilous for him to put himself in opposition to it, and it will be safer to follow the example of those around him and perhaps even "hunt with the pack." In obedience to the new authority he may put his former "conscience" out of action, and so surrender to the attraction of the increased pleasure that is certainly obtained from the removal of inhibitions. On the whole, therefore, it is not so remarkable that we should see an individual in a group doing or approving things which he would have avoided in the normal conditions of life; and in this way we may even hope to clear up a little of the obscurity which is so often covered by the enigmatic word "suggestion."

McDougall does not dispute the thesis as to the collective inhibition of intelligence in groups (ibid., 41). He says that the minds of lower intelligence bring down those of a higher order to their own level. The latter are obstructed in their activity, because in general an intensification of affect creates unfavorable conditions for sound intellectual work, and further because the individuals are intimidated by the group and their mental activity is not free, and because there is a lowering in each individual of his sense of responsibility for his own performances.

The judgment with which McDougall sums up the psychological behavior of a simple "unorganized" group is no more friendly than that of Le Bon. Such a group "is excessively emotional, impulsive, violent, fickle, inconsistent, irresolute and extreme in action, displaying only the coarser emotions and the less refined sentiments; extremely suggestible, careless in deliberation, hasty in judgment, incapable of any but the simpler and imperfect forms of reasoning; easily swayed and led, lacking in self-consciousness, devoid of self-respect and of sense of responsibility, and apt to be carried away by the consciousness of its own force, so that it tends to produce all the manifestations we have learned to expect of any irresponsible and absolute power. Hence its behavior is like that of an unruly child or an untutored passionate savage in a strange situation, rather than like that of its average member; and in the worst cases it is like that of a wild beast, rather than like that of human beings." (Ibid., 45.)

Since McDougall contrasts the behavior of a highly organized group with what has just been described, we shall be particularly interested to learn in what this organization consists, and by what factors it is produced. The author enumerates five "principal conditions" for raising collective mental life to a higher level.

The first and fundamental condition is that there should be some degree of continuity of existence in the group. This may be either material or formal: material, if the same individuals persist in the group for some time; and formal, if there is developed within the group a system of fixed positions which are occupied by a succession of individuals.

The second condition is that in the individual member of the group some definite idea should be formed of the nature, composition, functions and capacities of the group, so that from this he may develop an emotional relation to the group as a whole.

The third is that the group should be brought into interaction (perhaps in the form of rivalry) with other groups similar to it but differing from it in many respects.

The fourth is that the group should possess traditions, customs and habits, and especially such as determine the relations of its members to one another.

The fifth is that the group should have a definite structure, expressed in the specialization and differentiation of the functions of its constituents.

According to McDougall, if these conditions are fulfilled, the psychological disadvantages of group formations are removed. The collective lowering of intellectual ability is avoided by withdrawing the performance of intellectual tasks from the group and reserving them for individual members of it.

It seems to us that the condition which McDougall designates as the "organization" of a group can with more justification be described in another way. The problem consists in how to procure for the group precisely those features which were characteristic of the individual and which are extinguished in him by the formation of the group. For the individual, outside the primitive group, possessed his own continuity, his self-consciousness, his traditions and customs, his own particular functions and position, and he kept apart from his rivals. Owing to his entry into an "unorganized" group he had lost this distinctiveness for a time. If we thus recognize that the aim is to equip the group with the attributes of the individual, we shall be reminded of a valuable remark of Trotter's,[1] to the effect that the tendency toward the formation of groups is biologically a continuation of the multicellular character of all the higher organisms.[2]

*[handwritten note]*

Give the group the attributes
of the individual —
  ① Continuity —
  ② Self-Awareness
  ③ Tradition, Customs —
  ④ Function, Position —
  ⑤

[1] *Instincts of the Herd in Peace and War* (1916). [See below, p. 63 ff.]

[2] [*Footnote added* 1923:] I differ from what is in other respects an understanding and shrewd criticism by Hans Kelsen (1922) [of the present work] when he says that to provide the "group mind" with an organization of this kind signifies a hypostasis of it—that is to say, implies an attribution to it of independence of the mental processes in the individual.

# IV

## SUGGESTION AND LIBIDO

WE started from the fundamental fact that an individual in a group is subjected through its influence to what is often a profound alteration in his mental activity. His liability to affect becomes extraordinarily intensified, while his intellectual ability is markedly reduced, both processes being evidently in the direction of an approximation to the other individuals in the group; and this result can only be reached by the removal of those inhibitions upon his instincts which are peculiar to each individual, and by his resigning those expressions of his inclinations which are especially his own. We have heard that these often unwelcome consequences are to some extent at least prevented by a higher "organization" of the group; but this does not contradict the fundamental fact of group psychology—the two theses as to the intensification of the affects and the inhibition of the intellect in primitive groups. Our interest is now directed to discovering the psychological explanation of this mental change which is experienced by the individual in a group.

It is clear that rational factors (such as the intimidation of the individual which has already been mentioned, that is, the action of his instinct of self-preservation) do not cover the observable phenomena. Beyond this what we are offered as an explanation by authorities on sociology and group psychology is always the same, even though it is given various names, and

26

that is—the magic word "suggestion." Tarde [1890] calls it "imitation"; but we cannot help agreeing with a writer who protests that imitation comes under the concept of suggestion, and is in fact one of its results (Brugeilles, 1913). Le Bon traces back all the puzzling features of social phenomena to two factors: the mutual suggestion of individuals and the prestige of leaders. But prestige, again, is only recognizable by its capacity for evoking suggestion. McDougall for a moment gives us an impression that his principle of "primitive induction of emotion" might enable us to do without the assumption of suggestion. But on further consideration we are forced to perceive that this principle makes no more than the familiar assertions about "imitation" or "contagion," except for a decided stress upon the emotional factor. There is no doubt that something exists in us which, when we become aware of signs of an emotion in someone else, tends to make us fall into the same emotion; but how often do we not successfully oppose it, resist the emotion, and react in quite an opposite way? Why, therefore, do we invariably give way to this contagion when we are in a group? Once more we should have to say that what compels us to obey this tendency is imitation, and what induces the emotion in us is the group's suggestive influence. Moreover, quite apart from this, McDougall does not enable us to evade suggestion; we hear from him as well as from other writers that groups are distinguished by their special suggestibility.

We shall therefore be prepared for the statement that suggestion (or more correctly suggestibility) is actually an irreducible, primitive phenomenon, a fundamental fact in the mental life of man. Such, too, was the opinion of Bernheim, of whose astonishing arts I was a witness in the year 1889. But I can remember even then feeling a muffled hostility to this tyranny of suggestion. When a patient who showed himself unamenable was met with the shout: "What are you doing? *Vous vous contre-suggestionnez!,*" I said to my-self that this was an evident injustice and an act of violence. For the man certainly had a right to counter-suggestions if people were trying to subdue him with suggestions. Later on my resistance took the direction of protesting against the view that suggestion, which explained everything, was itself to be exempt from explanation.[1] Thinking of it, I repeated the old conundrum:[2]

> Christoph trug Christum,
> Christus trug die ganze Welt,
> Sag' wo hat Christoph
> Damals hin den Fuss gestellt?

> Christophorus Christum, sed Christus sustulit orbem:
> Constiterit pedibus dic ubi Christophorus?[3]

Now that I once more approach the riddle of suggestion after having kept away from it for some thirty years, I find there is no change in the situation. (There is one exception to be made to this statement, and one which bears witness precisely to the influence of psychoanalysis.) I notice that particular efforts are being made to formulate the concept of suggestion correctly, that is, to fix the conventional use of the name (e.g. McDougall, 1920). And this is by no means super-fluous, for the word is acquiring a more and more extended use and a looser and looser meaning [in German], and will soon come to designate any sort of influence whatever, just as it does in English, where "to suggest" and "suggestion" correspond to our *nahelegen* and *Anregung*. But there has been no ex-planation of the nature of suggestion, that is, of the

[1] [ See, for instance, some remarks in Freud's case history of "Little Hans" (1909), *Standard Ed.*, **10**, 102.]

[2] Konrad Richter, "Der deutsche S. Christoph."

[3] [Literally: "Christopher bore Christ; Christ bore the whole world; Say, where did Christopher then put his foot?"]

conditions under which influence without adequate logical foundation takes place. I should not avoid the task of supporting this statement by an analysis of the literature of the last thirty years, if I were not aware that an exhaustive inquiry is being undertaken close at hand which has in view the fulfillment of this very task.[1]

Instead of this I shall make an attempt at using the concept of *libido* for the purpose of throwing light upon group psychology, a concept which has done us such good service in the study of psychoneuroses.

Libido is an expression taken from the theory of the emotions. We call by that name the energy, regarded as a quantitative magnitude (though not at present actually measurable), of those instincts which have to do with all that may be comprised under the word "love." The nucleus of what we mean by love naturally consists (and this is what is commonly called love, and what the poets sing of) in sexual love with sexual union as its aim. But we do not separate from this—what in any case has a share in the name "love"—on the one hand, self-love, and on the other, love for parents and children, friendship and love for humanity in general, and also devotion to concrete objects and to abstract ideas. Our justification lies in the fact that psychoanalytic research has taught us that all these tendencies are an expression of the same instinctual impulses; in relations between the sexes these impulses force their way toward sexual union, but in other circumstances they are diverted from this aim or are prevented from reaching it, though always preserving enough of their original nature to keep their identity recognizable (as in such features as the longing for proximity, and self-sacrifice).

We are of opinion, then, that language has carried

1 [*Footnote added* 1925:] This work has unfortunately not materialized.

out an entirely justifiable piece of unification in cre-
ating the word "love" with its numerous uses, and that
we cannot do better than take it as the basis of our
scientific discussions and expositions as well. By coming to this decision, psychoanalysis has let loose a
storm of indignation, as though it had been guilty of
an act of outrageous innovation. Yet it has done nothing original in taking love in this "wider" sense. In its
origin, function, and relation to sexual love, the "Eros"
of the philosopher Plato coincides exactly with the
love-force, the libido of psychoanalysis, as has been
shown in detail by Nachmansohn (1915) and Pfister
(1921); and when the apostle Paul, in his famous
epistle to the Corinthians, praises love above all else,
he certainly understands it in the same "wider" sense.[1]
But this only shows that men do not always take their
great thinkers seriously, even when they profess most
to admire them.

Psychoanalysis, then, gives these love instincts the
name of sexual instincts, *a potiori* and by reason of
their origin. The majority of "educated" people have
regarded this nomenclature as an insult, and have
taken their revenge by retorting upon psychoanalysis
with the reproach of "pan-sexualism." Anyone who
considers sex as something mortifying and humiliating
to human nature is at liberty to make use of the more
genteel expressions "Eros" and "erotic." I might have
done so myself from the first and thus have spared
myself much opposition. But I did not want to, for I
like to avoid concessions to faintheartedness. One can
never tell where that road may lead one; one gives
way first in words, and then little by little in substance
too. I cannot see any merit in being ashamed of sex;
the Greek word "Eros," which is to soften the affront,
is in the end nothing more than a translation of our

[1] "Though I speak with the tongues of men and of angels, and
have not charity [love], I am become as sounding brass, or a
tinkling cymbal."

German word *Liebe* [love]; and finally, he who knows how to wait need make no concessions.

We will try our fortune, then, with the supposition that love relationships (or, to use a more neutral expression, emotional ties) also constitute the essence of the group mind. Let us remember that the authorities make no mention of any such relations. What would correspond to them is evidently concealed behind the shelter, the screen, of suggestion. Our hypothesis finds support in the first instance from two passing thoughts. First, that a group is clearly held together by a power of some kind: and to what power could this feat be better ascribed than to Eros, which holds together everything in the world?[1] Secondly, that if an individual gives up his distinctiveness in a group and lets its other members influence him by suggestion, it gives one the impression that he does it because he feels the need of being in harmony with them rather than in opposition to them—so that perhaps after all he does it *"ihnen zu Liebe."*[2]

---

[1] [See *Beyond the Pleasure Principle*, 1920, *Standard Ed.*, **18**; Bantam Classics Ed., *FC49*.]

[2] [An idiom meaning "for their sake." Literally: "for love of them."—A line of thought similar to that expressed in the last three paragraphs will be found in the almost contemporary Preface to the Fourth Edition of Freud's *Three Essays* (1905), *Standard Ed.*, **7**, 134.]

# V

## TWO ARTIFICIAL GROUPS: THE CHURCH AND THE ARMY

We may recall from what we know of the morphology of groups that it is possible to distinguish very different kinds of groups and opposing lines in their development. There are very fleeting groups and extremely lasting ones; homogeneous ones, made up of the same sorts of individuals, and unhomogeneous ones; natural groups, and artificial ones, requiring an external force to keep them together; primitive groups, and highly organized ones with a definite structure. But for reasons which remain to be explained we should like to lay particular stress upon a distinction to which writers on the subject have been inclined to give too little attention; I refer to that between leaderless groups and those with leaders. And, in complete opposition to the usual practice, we shall not choose a relatively simple group formation as our point of departure, but shall begin with highly organized, lasting and artificial groups. The most interesting example of such structures are Churches—communities of believers—and armies.

A Church and an army are artificial groups—that is, a certain external force is employed to prevent them from disintegrating[1] and to check alterations in their structure. As a rule a person is not consulted, or is

---

[1] [*Footnote added* 1923:] In groups, the attributes "stable" and "artificial" seem to coincide or at least to be intimately connected.

given no choice, as to whether he wants to enter such a group; any attempt at leaving it is usually met with persecution or with severe punishment, or has quite definite conditions attached to it. It is quite outside our present interest to inquire why these associations need such special safeguards. We are only attracted by one circumstance, namely that certain facts, which are far more concealed in other cases, can be observed very clearly in those highly organized groups which are protected from dissolution in the manner that has been mentioned.

In a Church (and we may with advantage take the Catholic Church as a type) as well as in an army, however different the two may be in other respects, the same illusion holds good of there being a head—in the Catholic Church Christ, in an army its Commander-in-Chief—who loves all the individuals in the group with an equal love. Everything depends upon this illusion; if it were to be dropped, then both Church and army would dissolve, so far as the external force permitted them to. This equal love was expressly enunciated by Christ: "Inasmuch as ye have done it unto one of the least of these my brethren, ye have done it unto me." He stands to the individual members of the group of believers in the relation of a kind elder brother; he is their substitute father. All the demands that are made upon the individual are derived from this love of Christ's. A democratic strain runs through the Church, for the very reason that before Christ everyone is equal, and that everyone has an equal share in his love. It is not without a deep reason that the similarity between the Christian community and a family is invoked, and that believers call themselves brothers in Christ, that is, brothers through the love which Christ has for them. There is no doubt that the tie which unites each individual with Christ is also the cause of the tie which unites them with one another. The like holds good of an army. The Commander-in-

Chief is a father who loves all soldiers equally, and for that reason they are comrades among themselves. The army differs structurally from the Church in being built up of a series of such groups. Every captain is, as it were, the Commander-in-Chief and the father of his company, and so is every non-commissioned officer of his section. It is true that a similar hierarchy has been constructed in the Church, but it does not play the same part in it economically;[1] for more knowledge and care about individuals may be attributed to Christ than to a human Commander-in-Chief.

An objection will justly be raised against this conception of the libidinal structure of an army on the ground that no place has been found in it for such ideas as those of one's country, of national glory, etc., which are of such importance in holding an army together. The answer is that that is a different instance of a group tie, and no longer such a simple one; for the examples of great generals, like Caesar, Wallenstein, or Napoleon, show that such ideas are not indispensable to the existence of an army. We shall presently touch upon the possibility of a leading idea being substituted for a leader and upon the relations between the two. The neglect of this libidinal factor in an army, even when it is not the only factor operative, seems to be not merely a theoretical omission but also a practical danger. Prussian militarism, which was just as unpsychological as German science, may have had to suffer the consequences of this in the [first] World War. We know that the war neuroses which ravaged the German army have been recognized as being a protest of the individual against the part he was expected to play in the army; and according to the communication of Simmel (1918), the hard treatment of the men by their superiors may be considered as foremost among the motive forces of the

1 [i.e. in the quantitative distribution of the psychical forces involved.]

disease. If the importance of the libido's claims on this score had been better appreciated, the fantastic promises of the American President's Fourteen Points would probably not have been believed so easily, and the splendid instrument would not have broken in the hands of the German leaders.[1]

It is to be noticed that in these two artificial groups each individual is bound by libidinal ties on the one hand to the leader (Christ, the Commander-in-Chief) and on the other hand to the other members of the group. How these two ties are related to each other, whether they are of the same kind and the same value, and how they are to be described psychologically—these questions must be reserved for subsequent inquiry. But we shall venture even now upon a mild reproach against earlier writers for not having sufficiently appreciated the importance of the leader in the psychology of the group, while our own choice of this as a first subject for investigation has brought us into a more favorable position. It would appear as though we were on the right road toward an explanation of the principal phenomenon of group psychology —the individual's lack of freedom in a group. If each individual is bound in two directions by such an intense emotional tie, we shall find no difficulty in attributing to that circumstance the alteration and limitation which have been observed in his personality.

A hint to the same effect, that the essence of a group lies in the libidinal ties existing in it, is also to be found in the phenomenon of panic, which is best studied in military groups. A panic arises if a group of that kind becomes disintegrated. Its characteristics are that none of the orders given by superiors are any longer listened to, and that each individual is only

[1] [By Freud's wish this paragraph was printed as a footnote in the English translation of 1922. It appears in the text in all the German editions, however, both before and after that date. See Editor's Note, p. 1.]

solicitous on his own account, and without any consideration for the rest. The mutual ties have ceased to exist, and a gigantic and senseless fear is set free. At this point, again, the objection will naturally be made that it is rather the other way round; and that the fear has grown so great as to be able to disregard all ties and all feelings of consideration for others. McDougall (1920, 24) has even made use of panic (though not of military panic) as a typical instance of that intensification of emotion by contagion ("primary induction") on which he lays so much emphasis. But nevertheless this rational method of explanation is here quite inadequate. The very question that needs explanation is why the fear has become so gigantic. The greatness of the danger cannot be responsible, for the same army which now falls a victim to panic may previously have faced equally great or greater danger with complete success; it is of the very essence of panic that it bears no relation to the danger that threatens, and often breaks out on the most trivial occasions. If an individual in panic fear begins to be solicitous only on his own account, he bears witness in so doing to the fact that the emotional ties, which have hitherto made the danger seem small to him, have ceased to exist. Now that he is by himself in facing the danger, he may surely think it greater. The fact is, therefore, that panic fear presupposes a relaxation in the libidinal structure of the group and reacts to that relaxation in a justifiable manner, and the contrary view—that the libidinal ties of the group are destroyed owing to fear in the face of the danger—can be refuted.

The contention that fear in a group is increased to enormous proportions through induction (contagion) is not in the least contradicted by these remarks. McDougall's view meets the case entirely when the danger is a really great one and when the group has no strong emotional ties—conditions which are fulfilled, for instance, when a fire breaks out in a theatre or a place of amusement. But the truly instructive case and the one which can be best employed for our purposes is that mentioned above, in which a body of troops breaks into a panic although the danger has not increased beyond a degree that is usual and has often been previously faced. It is not to be expected that the usage of the word "panic" should be clearly and unambiguously determined. Sometimes it is used to describe any collective fear, sometimes even fear in an individual when it exceeds all bounds, and often the name seems to be reserved for cases in which the outbreak of fear is not warranted by the occasion. If we take the word "panic" in the sense of collective fear, we can establish a far-reaching analogy. Fear in an individual is provoked either by the greatness of a danger or by the cessation of emotional ties (libidinal cathexes); the latter is the case of neurotic fear or anxiety.[1] In just the same way panic arises either owing to an increase of the common danger or owing to the disappearance of the emotional ties which hold the group together; and the latter case is analogous to that of neurotic anxiety.[2]

Anyone who, like McDougall (1920), describes a panic as one of the plainest functions of the "group mind," arrives at the paradoxical position that this group mind does away with itself in one of its most striking manifestations. It is impossible to doubt that panic means the disintegration of a group; it involves the cessation of all the feelings of consideration which the members of the group otherwise show one another.

The typical occasion of the outbreak of a panic is very much as it is represented in Nestroy's parody of Hebbel's play about Judith and Holofernes. A soldier cries out: "The general has lost his head!" and there-

[1] See Lecture XXV of my *Introductory Lectures* (1916–17). [See also, however, *Inhibitions, Symptoms and Anxiety* (1926).]

[2] Compare Béla von Felszeghy's interesting though somewhat overimaginative paper "Panik und Pankomplex" (1920).

upon all the Assyrians take to flight. The loss of the leader in some sense or other, the birth of misgivings about him, brings on the outbreak of panic, though the danger remains the same; the mutual ties between the members of the group disappear, as a rule, at the same time as the tie with their leader. The group vanishes in dust, like a Prince Rupert's drop when its tail is broken off.

The dissolution of a religious group is not so easy to observe. A short time ago there came into my hands an English novel of Catholic origin, recommended by the Bishop of London, with the title *When It Was Dark*.[1] It gave a clever and, as it seems to me, a convincing picture of such a possibility and its consequences. The novel, which is supposed to relate to the present day, tells how a conspiracy of enemies of the person of Christ and of the Christian faith succeed in arranging for a sepulchre to be discovered in Jerusalem. In this sepulchre is an inscription, in which Joseph of Arimathaea confesses that for reasons of piety he secretly removed the body of Christ from its grave on the third day after its entombment and buried it in this spot. The resurrection of Christ and his divine nature are by this means disproved, and the result of this archaeological discovery is a convulsion in European civilization and an extraordinary increase in all crimes and acts of violence, which only ceases when the forgers' plot has been revealed.

The phenomenon which accompanies the dissolution that is here supposed to overtake a religious group is not fear, for which the occasion is wanting. Instead of it ruthless and hostile impulses toward other people make their appearance, which, owing to the equal love of Christ, they had previously been unable

1 [A book by "Guy Thorne" (pseudonym of C. Ranger Gull) which enjoyed extremely large sales at the time of its publication in 1903.]

to do.[1] But even during the kingdom of Christ those people who do not belong to the community of believers, who do not love him, and whom he does not love, stand outside this tie. Therefore a religion, even if it calls itself the religion of love, must be hard and unloving to those who do not belong to it. Fundamentally indeed every religion is in this same way a religion of love for all those whom it embraces; while cruelty and intolerance toward those who do not belong to it are natural to every religion. However difficult we may find it personally, we ought not to reproach believers too severely on this account; people who are unbelieving or indifferent are much better off psychologically in this matter [of cruelty and intolerance]. If today that intolerance no longer shows itself so violent and cruel as in former centuries, we can scarcely conclude that there has been a softening in human manners. The cause is rather to be found in the undeniable weakening of religious feelings and the libidinal ties which depend upon them. If another group tie takes the place of the religious one—and the socialistic tie seems to be succeeding in doing so— then there will be the same intolerance toward outsiders as in the age of the Wars of Religion; and if differences between scientific opinions could ever attain a similar significance for groups, the same result would again be repeated with this new motivation.

[1] Compare the explanation of similar phenomena after the abolition of the paternal authority of the sovereign given in Federn's *Die vaterlose Gesellschaft* (1919).

# VI

## FURTHER PROBLEMS AND LINES OF WORK

WE have hitherto considered two artificial groups and have found that both are dominated by emotional ties of two kinds. One of these, the tie with the leader, seems (at all events for these cases) to be more of a ruling factor than the other, which holds between the members of the group.

Now much else remains to be examined and described in the morphology of groups. We should have to start from the ascertained fact that a mere collection of people is not a group, so long as these ties have not been established in it; but we should have to admit that in any collection of people the tendency to form a psychological group may very easily come to the fore. We should have to give our attention to the different kinds of groups, more or less stable, that arise spontaneously, and to study the conditions of their origin and of their dissolution. We should above all be concerned with the distinction between groups which have a leader and leaderless groups. We should consider whether groups with leaders may not be the more primitive and complete, whether in the others an idea, an abstraction, may not take the place of the leader (a state of things to which religious groups, with their invisible head, form a transitional stage), and whether a common tendency, a wish in which a number of people can have a share, may not in the same way serve as a substitute. This abstraction, again, might be more or less completely embodied in the figure of what we might call a secondary leader, and interesting varieties would arise from the relation between the idea and the leader. The leader or the leading idea might also, so to speak, be negative; hatred against a particular person or institution might operate in just the same unifying way, and might call up the same kind of emotional ties as positive attachment. Then the question would also arise whether a leader is really indispensable to the essence of a group —and other questions besides.

But all these questions, which may, moreover, have been dealt with in part in the literature of group psychology, will not succeed in diverting our interest from the fundamental psychological problems that confront us in the structure of a group. And our attention will first be attracted by a consideration which promises to bring us in the most direct way to a proof that libidinal ties are what characterize a group.

Let us keep before our eyes the nature of the emotional relations which hold between men in general. According to Schopenhauer's famous simile of the freezing porcupines no one can tolerate a too intimate approach to his neighbor.[1]

The evidence of psychoanalysis shows that almost every intimate emotional relation between two people which lasts for some time—marriage, friendship, the

[1] "A company of porcupines crowded themselves very close together one cold winter's day so as to profit by one another's warmth and so save themselves from being frozen to death. But soon they felt one another's quills, which induced them to separate again. And now, when the need for warmth brought them nearer together again, the second evil arose once more. So that they were driven backwards and forwards from one trouble to the other, until they had discovered a mean distance at which they could most tolerably exist." (*Parerga und Paralipomena,* Part II, 31, "Gleichnisse und Parabeln.")

relations between parents and children[1]—leaves a sediment of feelings of aversion and hostility, which only escapes perception as a result of repression.[2] This is less disguised in the common wrangles between business partners or in the grumbles of a subordinate at his superior. The same thing happens when men come together in larger units. Every time two families become connected by a marriage, each of them thinks itself superior to or of better birth than the other. Of two neighboring towns each is the other's most jealous rival; every little canton looks down upon the others with contempt. Closely related races keep one another at arm's length; the South German cannot endure the North German, the Englishman casts every kind of aspersion upon the Scot, the Spaniard despises the Portuguese.[3] We are no longer astonished that greater differences should lead to an almost insuperable repugnance, such as the Gallic people feel for the German, the Aryan for the Semite, and the white races for the colored.

When this hostility is directed against people who are otherwise loved we describe it as ambivalence of feeling; and we explain the fact, in what is probably far too rational a manner, by means of the numerous occasions for conflicts of interest which arise precisely in such intimate relations. In the undisguised antipathies and aversions which people feel toward strangers with whom they have to do we may recognize the expression of self-love—of narcissism. This self-love works for the preservation of the individual, and behaves as though the occurrence of any divergence

[1] Perhaps with the solitary exception of the relation of a mother to her son, which is based on narcissism, is not disturbed by subsequent rivalry, and is reinforced by a rudimentary attempt at sexual object-choice.

[2] [In the first German edition the last clause read "which has first to be eliminated by repression." It was amended in 1923.]

[3] ["The narcissism of minor differences," Chapter V of Freud, 1930.]

from his own particular lines of development involved a criticism of them and a demand for their alteration. We do not know why such sensitiveness should have been directed to just these details of differentiation; but it is unmistakable that in this whole connection men give evidence of a readiness for hatred, an aggressiveness, the source of which is unknown, and to which one is tempted to ascribe an elementary character.[1]

But when a group is formed the whole of this intolerance vanishes, temporarily or permanently, within the group. So long as a group formation persists or so far as it extends, individuals in the group behave as though they were uniform, tolerate the peculiarities of its other members, equate themselves with them, and have no feeling of aversion toward them. Such a limitation of narcissism can, according to our theoretical views, only be produced by one factor, a libidinal tie with other people. Love for oneself knows only one barrier—love for others, love for objects.[2] The question will at once be raised whether community of interest in itself, without any addition of libido, must not necessarily lead to the toleration of other people and to considerateness for them. This objection may be met by the reply that nevertheless no lasting limitation of narcissism is effected in this way, since this tolerance does not persist longer than the immediate advantage gained from the other people's collaboration. But the practical importance of this discussion is less than might be supposed, for experience has shown that in cases of collaboration libidinal ties are regularly formed between the fellow-workers

---

[1] In a recently published study, *Beyond the Pleasure Principle* [1920], I have attempted to connect the polarity of love and hatred with a hypothetical opposition between instincts of life and death, and to establish the sexual instincts as the purest examples of the former, the instincts of life.

[2] See my paper on narcissism (1914).

which prolong and solidify the relation between them to a point beyond what is merely profitable. The same thing occurs in men's social relations as has become familiar to psychoanalytic research in the course of the development of the individual libido. The libido attaches itself to the satisfaction of the great vital needs, and chooses as its first objects the people who have a share in that process.[1] And in the development of mankind as a whole, just as in individuals, love alone acts as the civilizing factor in the sense that it brings a change from egoism to altruism. And this is true both of sexual love for women, with all the obligations which it involves of not harming the things that are dear to women, and also of desexualized, sublimated homosexual love for other men, which springs from work in common.

If therefore in groups narcissistic self-love is subject to limitations which do not operate outside them, that is cogent evidence that the essence of a group formation consists in new kinds of libidinal ties among the members of the group.

Our interest now leads us on to the pressing question as to what may be the nature of these ties which exist in groups. In the psychoanalytic study of neuroses we have hitherto been occupied almost exclusively with ties with objects made by love instincts which still pursue directly sexual aims. In groups there can evidently be no question of sexual aims of that kind. We are concerned here with love instincts which have been diverted from their original aims, though they do not operate with less energy on that account. Now, within the range of the usual sexual object-cathexis, we have already observed phenomena which represent a diversion of the instinct from its sexual aim. We have described them as degrees of being in love, and have recognized that they involve a certain

[1] [See Section 5 of the third of Freud's *Three Essays* (1905), *Standard Ed.*, 7, 222.]

encroachment upon the ego. We shall now turn our attention more closely to these phenomena of being in love, in the firm expectation of finding in them conditions which can be transferred to the ties that exist in groups. But we should also like to know whether this kind of object-cathexis, as we know it in sexual life, represents the only manner of emotional tie with other people, or whether we must take other mechanisms of the sort into account. As a matter of fact we learn from psychoanalysis that there do exist other mechanisms for emotional ties, the so-called *identifications*,[1] insufficiently-known processes and hard to describe, the investigation of which will for some time keep us away from the subject of group psychology.

[1] [Freud had discussed identification, though less fully, in Chapter IV of *The Interpretation of Dreams* (1900), *Standard Ed.*, 4, 149–151, and "Mourning and Melancholia" (1917). The subject is already touched on in the Fliess correspondence, e.g. in Draft N of May 31, 1897 (Freud, 1950).]

# VII

## IDENTIFICATION

IDENTIFICATION is known to psychoanalysis as the earliest expression of an emotional tie with another person. It plays a part in the early history of the Oedipus complex. A little boy will exhibit a special interest in his father; he would like to grow like him and be like him, and take his place everywhere. We may say simply that he takes his father as his ideal. This behavior has nothing to do with a passive or feminine attitude toward his father (and toward males in general); it is on the contrary typically masculine. It fits in very well with the Oedipus complex, for which it helps to prepare the way.

At the same time as this identification with his father, or a little later, the boy has begun to develop a true object-cathexis toward his mother according to the attachment [anaclitic] type.[1] He then exhibits, therefore, two psychologically distinct ties: a straightforward sexual object-cathexis toward his mother and an identification with his father which takes him as his model. The two subsist side by side for a time without any mutual influence or interference. In consequence of the irresistible advance toward a unification of mental life, they come together at last; and the normal Oedipus complex originates from their confluence. The little boy notices that his father stands in his way with his mother. His identification with his father

1 [See Section II of Freud's paper on narcissism (1914).]

then takes on a hostile coloring and becomes identical with the wish to replace his father in regard to his mother as well. Identification, in fact, is ambivalent from the very first; it can turn into an expression of tenderness as easily as into a wish for someone's removal. It behaves like a derivative of the first, *oral* phase of the organization of the libido, in which the object that we long for and prize is assimilated by eating and is in that way annihilated as such. The cannibal, as we know, has remained at this standpoint; he has a devouring affection for his enemies and only devours people of whom he is fond.[1]

The subsequent history of this identification with the father may easily be lost sight of. It may happen that the Oedipus complex becomes inverted, and that the father is taken as the object of a feminine attitude, an object from which the directly sexual instincts look for satisfaction; in that event the identification with the father has become the precursor of an object-tie with the father. The same holds good, with the necessary substitutions, of the baby daughter as well.[2]

It is easy to state in a formula the distinction between an identification with the father and the choice of the father as an object. In the first case one's father is what one would like to *be*, and in the second he is what one would like to *have*. The distinction, that is, depends upon whether the tie attaches to the subject or to the object of the ego. The former kind of tie is therefore already possible before any sexual object-choice has been made. It is much more difficult to give a clear metapsychological representation of the distinction. We can only see that identification endeavors to mold a person's own ego after the fashion of the one that has been taken as a model.

[1] See my *Three Essays* (1905) [*Standard Ed.*, 7, 198].
[2] [The "complete" Oedipus complex, comprising both its "positive" and its "negative" forms, is discussed by Freud in Chapter III of *The Ego and the Id* (1923).]

Let us disentangle identification as it occurs in the structure of a neurotic symptom from its rather complicated connections. Supposing that a little girl (and we will keep to her for the present) develops the same painful symptom as her mother—for instance, the same tormenting cough. This may come about in various ways. The identification may come from the Oedipus complex; in that case it signifies a hostile desire on the girl's part to take her mother's place, and the symptom expresses her object-love toward her father, and brings about a realization, under the influence of a sense of guilt, of her desire to take her mother's place: "You wanted to be your mother, and now you *are*—anyhow so far as your sufferings are concerned." This is the complete mechanism of the structure of a hysterical symptom. Or, on the other hand, the symptom may be the same as that of the person who is loved; so, for instance, Dora[1] imitated her father's cough. In that case we can only describe the state of things by saying *that identification has appeared instead of object-choice, and that object-choice has regressed to identification.* We have heard that identification is the earliest and original form of emotional tie; it often happens that under the conditions in which symptoms are constructed, that is, where there is repression and where the mechanisms of the unconscious are dominant, object-choice is turned back into identification—the ego assumes the characteristics of the object. It is noticeable that in these identifications the ego sometimes copies the person who is not loved and sometimes the one who is loved. It must also strike us that in both cases the identification is a partial and extremely limited one and only borrows a single trait from the person who is its object.

There is a third particularly frequent and important

[1] In my "Fragment of an Analysis of a Case of Hysteria" (1905) *Standard Ed.,* **7,** 82–3].

case of symptom formation, in which the identification leaves entirely out of account any object-relation to the person who is being copied. Supposing, for instance, that one of the girls in a boarding school has had a letter from someone with whom she is secretly in love which arouses her jealousy, and that she reacts to it with a fit of hysterics; then some of her friends who know about it will catch the fit, as we say, by mental infection. The mechanism is that of identification based upon the possibility or desire of putting oneself in the same situation. The other girls would like to have a secret love affair too, and under the influence of a sense of guilt they also accept the suffering involved in it. It would be wrong to suppose that they take on the symptom out of sympathy. On the contrary, the sympathy only arises out of the identification, and this is proved by the fact that infection or imitation of this kind takes place in circumstances where even less pre-existing sympathy is to be assumed than usually exists between friends in a girls' school. One ego has perceived a significant analogy with another upon one point—in our example upon openness to a similar emotion; an identification is thereupon constructed on this point, and, under the influence of the pathogenic situation, is displaced on to the symptom which the one ego has produced. The identification by means of the symptom has thus become the mark of a point of coincidence between the two egos which has to be kept repressed.

What we have learned from these three sources may be summarized as follows. First, identification is the original form of emotional tie with an object; secondly, in a regressive way it becomes a substitute for a libidinal object-tie, as it were by means of introjection of the object into the ego; and thirdly, it may arise with any new perception of a common quality shared with some other person who is not an object of the sexual instinct. The more important this common quality is, the more successful may this partial identification become, and it may thus represent the beginning of a new tie.

We already begin to divine that the mutual tie between members of a group is in the nature of an identification of this kind, based upon an important emotional common quality; and we may suspect that this common quality lies in the nature of the tie with the leader. Another suspicion may tell us that we are far from having exhausted the problem of identification, and that we are faced by the process which psychology calls "empathy [*Einfühlung*]" and which plays the largest part in our understanding of what is inherently foreign to our ego in other people. But we shall here limit ourselves to the immediate emotional effects of identification, and shall leave on one side its significance for our intellectual life.

Psychoanalytic research, which has already occasionally attacked the more difficult problems of the psychoses, has also been able to exhibit identification to us in some other cases which are not immediately comprehensible. I shall treat two of these cases in detail as material for further consideration.

The genesis of male homosexuality in a large class of cases is as follows.[1] A young man has been unusually long and intensely fixated upon his mother in the sense of the Oedipus complex. But at last, after the end of puberty, the time comes for exchanging his mother for some other sexual object. Things take a sudden turn: the young man does not abandon his mother, but identifies himself with her; he transforms himself into her, and now looks about for objects which can replace his ego for him, and on which he can bestow such love and care as he has experienced from his mother. This is a frequent process, which can be con-

[1] [See Chapter III of Freud's study on Leonardo (1910).]

firmed as often as one likes, and which is naturally quite independent of any hypothesis that may be made as to the organic driving force and the motives of the sudden transformation. A striking thing about this identification is its ample scale; it remolds the ego in one of its important features—in its sexual character —upon the model of what has hitherto been the object. In this process the object itself is renounced— whether entirely or in the sense of being preserved only in the unconscious is a question outside the present discussion. Identification with an object that is renounced or lost, as a substitute for that object— introjection of it into the ego—is indeed no longer a novelty to us. A process of the kind may sometimes be observed in small children. A short time ago an observation of this sort was published in the *Internationale Zeitschrift für Psychoanalyse*. A child who was unhappy over the loss of a kitten declared straight out that now he himself was the kitten, and accordingly crawled about on all fours, would not eat at table, etc.[1]

Another such instance of introjection of the object has been provided by the analysis of melancholia,[2] an affection which counts among the most notable of its exciting causes the real or emotional loss of a loved object. A leading characteristic of these cases is a cruel self-depreciation of the ego combined with relentless self-criticism and bitter self-reproaches. Analyses have shown that this disparagement and these reproaches apply at bottom to the object and represent the ego's revenge upon it. The shadow of the object has fallen upon the ego, as I have said elsewhere.[3] The introjection of the object is here unmistakably clear.

But these melancholias also show us something else,

---

[1] Marcuszewicz (1920).

[2] [Freud habitually uses the term "melancholia" for conditions which would now be described as "depression."]

[3] See "Mourning and Melancholia" (1917).

which may be of importance for our later discussions. They show us the ego divided, fallen apart into two pieces, one of which rages against the second. This second piece is the one which has been altered by introjection and which contains the lost object. But the piece which behaves so cruelly is not unknown to us either. It comprises the conscience, a critical agency within the ego, which even in normal times takes up a critical attitude toward the ego, though never so relentlessly and so unjustifiably. On previous occasions[1] we have been driven to the hypothesis that some such agency develops in our ego which may cut itself off from the rest of the ego and come into conflict with it. We have called it the "ego ideal," and by way of functions we have ascribed to it self-observation, the moral conscience, the censorship of dreams, and the chief influence in repression. We have said that it is the heir to the original narcissism in which the childish ego enjoyed self-sufficiency; it gradually gathers up from the influences of the environment the demands which that environment makes upon the ego and which the ego cannot always rise to; so that a man, when he cannot be satisfied with his ego itself, may nevertheless be able to find satisfaction in the ego ideal which has been differentiated out of the ego. In delusions of observation, as we have further shown, the disintegration of this agency has become patent, and has thus revealed its origin in the influence of superior powers, and above all of parents.[2] But we have not forgotten to add that the amount of distance between this ego ideal and the real ego is very variable from one individual to another, and that with many people this differentiation within the ego does not go further than with children.

[1] In my paper on narcissism (1914) and in "Mourning and Melancholia" (1917).
[2] Section III of my paper on narcissism.

But before we can employ this material for understanding the libidinal organization of groups, we must
take into account some other examples of the mutual
relations between the object and the ego.[1]

---

[1] We are very well aware that we have not exhausted the nature of identification with these examples taken from pathology,
and that we have consequently left part of the riddle of group
formations untouched. A far more fundamental and comprehensive psychological analysis would have to intervene at this point.
A path leads from identification by way of imitation to empathy, that is, to the comprehension of the mechanism by means
of which we are enabled to take up any attitude at all toward
another mental life. Moreover there is still much to be explained
in the manifestations of existing identifications. These result
among other things in a person limiting his aggressiveness toward those with whom he has identified himself, and in his
sparing them and giving them help. The study of such identifications, like those, for instance, which lie at the root of clan feeling, led Robertson Smith (*Kinship and Marriage*, 1885) to the
surprising discovery that they rest upon the acknowledgment
of the possession of a common substance [by the members of the
clan], and may even therefore be created by a meal eaten in
common. This feature makes it possible to connect this kind of
identification with the early history of the human family which
I constructed in *Totem and Taboo*.

# VIII

## BEING IN LOVE AND HYPNOSIS

EVEN in its caprices the usage of language remains true to some kind of reality. Thus it gives the name of "love" to a great many kinds of emotional relationship which we too group together theoretically as love; but then again it feels a doubt whether this love is real, true, actual love, and so hints at a whole scale of possibilities within the range of the phenomena of love. We shall have no difficulty in making the same discovery from our own observations.

In one class of cases being in love is nothing more than object-cathexis on the part of the sexual instincts with a view to directly sexual satisfaction, a cathexis which expires, moreover, when this aim has been reached; this is what is called common, sensual love. But, as we know, the libidinal situation rarely remains so simple. It was possible to calculate with certainty upon the revival of the need which had just expired; and this must no doubt have been the first motive for directing a lasting cathexis upon the sexual object and for "loving" it in the passionless intervals as well.

To this must be added another factor derived from the very remarkable course of development which is pursued by the erotic life of man. In its first phase, which has usually come to an end by the time a child is five years old, he has found the first object for his love in one or other of his parents, and all of his sexual instincts with their demand for satisfaction

have been united upon this object. The repression
which then sets in compels him to renounce the greater
number of these infantile sexual aims, and leaves behind a profound modification in his relation to his
parents. The child still remains tied to his parents,
but by instincts which must be described as being
"inhibited in their aim." The emotions which he feels
henceforward toward these objects of his love are characterized as "affectionate." It is well known that the
earlier "sensual" tendencies remain more or less
strongly preserved in the unconscious, so that in a
certain sense the whole of the original current con-
tinues to exist.[1]

At puberty, as we know, there set in new and very
strong impulsions toward directly sexual aims. In
unfavorable cases they remain separate, in the form of
a sensual current, from the "affectionate" trends of
feeling which persist. We then have before us a picture
whose two aspects are typified with such delight by
certain schools of literature. A man will show a sentimental enthusiasm for women whom he deeply respects
but who do not excite him to sexual activities, and
he will only be potent with other women whom he
does not "love" and thinks little of or even despises.[2]
More often, however, the adolescent succeeds in bringing about a certain degree of synthesis between the
unsensual, heavenly love and the sensual, earthly love,
and his relation to his sexual object is characterized
by the interaction of uninhibited instincts and of
instincts inhibited in their aim. The depth to which
anyone is in love, as contrasted with his purely sensual
desire, may be measured by the size of the share taken
by the aim-inhibited instincts of affection.

In connection with this question of being in love

[1] See my *Three Essays* (1905) [*Standard Ed.*, 7, 200].
[2] "On the Universal Tendency to Debasement in the Sphere
of Love" (1912).

we have always been struck by the phenomenon of sexual overvaluation—the fact that the loved object enjoys a certain amount of freedom from criticism, and that all its characteristics are valued more highly than those of people who are not loved, or than its own were at a time when it itself was not loved. If the sensual impulses are more or less effectively repressed or set aside, the illusion is produced that the object has come to be sensually loved on account of its spiritual merits, whereas on the contrary these merits may really only have been lent to it by its sensual charm.

The tendency which falsifies judgment in this respect is that of *idealization*. But now it is easier for us to find our bearings. We see that the object is being treated in the same way as our own ego, so that when we are in love a considerable amount of narcissistic libido overflows on to the object.[1] It is even obvious, in many forms of love-choice, that the object serves as a substitute for some unattained ego ideal of our own. We love it on account of the perfections which we have striven to reach for our own ego, and which we should now like to procure in this roundabout way as a means of satisfying our narcissism.

If the sexual overvaluation and the being in love increase even further, then the interpretation of the picture becomes still more unmistakable. The impulsions whose trend is toward directly sexual satisfaction may now be pushed into the background entirely, as regularly happens, for instance, with a young man's sentimental passion; the ego becomes more and more unassuming and modest, and the object more and more sublime and precious, until at last it gets possession of the entire self-love of the ego, whose self-sacrifice thus follows as a natural consequence. The

---

[1] [Cf. a passage toward the beginning of Part III of Freud's paper on narcissism (1914).]

object has, so to speak, consumed the ego. Traits of humility, of the limitation of narcissism, and of self-injury occur in every case of being in love; in the extreme case they are merely intensified, and as a result of the withdrawal of the sensual claims they remain in solitary supremacy.

This happens especially easily with love that is unhappy and cannot be satisfied; for in spite of everything each sexual satisfaction always involves a reduction in sexual overvaluation. Contemporaneously with this "devotion" of the ego to the object, which is no longer to be distinguished from a sublimated devotion to an abstract idea, the functions allotted to the ego ideal entirely cease to operate. The criticism exercised by that agency is silent; everything that the object does and asks for is right and blameless. Conscience has no application to anything that is done for the sake of the object; in the blindness of love remorselessness is carried to the pitch of crime. The whole situation can be completely summarized in a formula: *The object has been put in the place of the ego ideal.*

It is now easy to define the difference between identification and such extreme developments of being in love as may be described as "fascination" or "bondage."[1] In the former case the ego has enriched itself with the properties of the object, it has "introjected" the object into itself, as Ferenczi [1909] expresses it. In the second case it is impoverished, it has surrendered itself to the object, it has substituted the object for its own most important constituent. Closer consideration soon makes it plain, however, that this kind of account creates an illusion of contradistinctions that have no real existence. Economically there is no question of impoverishment or enrichment; it is even possible to describe an extreme case of being in love as a state

---

[1] [The "bondage" of love had been discussed by Freud in the early part of his paper on "The Taboo of Virginity" (1918).]

in which the ego has introjected the object into itself. Another distinction is perhaps better calculated to meet the essence of the matter. In the case of identification the object has been lost or given up; it is then set up again inside the ego, and the ego makes a partial alteration in itself after the model of the lost object. In the other case the object is retained; and there is a hypercathexis of it by the ego and at the ego's expense. But here again a difficulty presents itself. Is it quite certain that identification presupposes that object-cathexis has been given up? Can there be no identification while the object is retained? And before we embark upon a discussion of this delicate question, the perception may already be beginning to dawn on us that yet another alternative embraces the real essence of the matter, namely, *whether the object is put in the place of the ego or of the ego ideal.*

From being in love to hypnosis is evidently only a short step. The respects in which the two agree are obvious. There is the same humble subjection, the same compliance, the same absence of criticism, toward the hypnotist as toward the loved object.[1] There is the same sapping of the subject's own initiative; no one can doubt that the hypnotist has stepped into the place of the ego ideal. It is only that everything is even clearer and more intense in hypnosis, so that it would be more to the point to explain being in love by means of hypnosis than the other way round. The hypnotist is the sole object, and no attention is paid to any but him. The fact that the ego experiences in a dreamlike way whatever he may request or assert reminds us that we omitted to mention among the functions of the ego ideal the business of testing the

1 [This point had already been made in a footnote to the first of Freud's *Three Essays* (1905) *Standard Ed.*, 7, 150, and in his paper on "Psychical Treatment" (1905), ibid., 296.]

reality of things.[1] No wonder that the ego takes a perception for real if its reality is vouched for by the mental agency which ordinarily discharges the duty of testing the reality of things. The complete absence of impulsions which are uninhibited in their sexual aims contributes further toward the extreme purity of the phenomena. The hypnotic relation is the unlimited devotion of someone in love, but with sexual satisfaction excluded; whereas in the actual case of being in love this kind of satisfaction is only temporarily kept back, and remains in the background as a possible aim at some later time.

But on the other hand we may also say that the hypnotic relation is (if the expression is permissible) a group formation with two members. Hypnosis is not a good object for comparison with a group formation, because it is truer to say that it is identical with it. Out of the complicated fabric of the group it isolates one element for us—the behavior of the individual to the leader. Hypnosis is distinguished from a group formation by this limitation of number, just as it is distinguished from being in love by the absence of directly sexual trends. In this respect it occupies a middle position between the two.

It is interesting to see that it is precisely those sexual impulsions that are inhibited in their aims which achieve such lasting ties between people. But this can easily be understood from the fact that they are not capable of complete satisfaction, while sexual impulsions which are uninhibited in their aims suffer an extraordinary reduction through the discharge of energy every time the sexual aim is attained. It is the

1 [*Added* 1923:] There seems, however, to be some doubt whether the attribution of this function to the ego ideal is justified. The point requires thorough discussion. [See the footnote at the beginning of Chapter III of *The Ego and The Id* (1923), where the function is definitely attributed to the *ego*.]

fate of sensual love to become extinguished when it is satisfied; for it to be able to last, it must from the beginning be mixed with purely affectionate components—with such, that is, as are inhibited in their aims —or it must itself undergo a transformation of this kind.

Hypnosis would solve the riddle of the libidinal constitution of groups for us straight away, if it were not that it itself exhibits some features which are not met by the rational explanation we have hitherto given of it as a state of being in love with the directly sexual trends excluded. There is still a great deal in it which we must recognize as unexplained and mysterious. It contains an additional element of paralysis derived from the relation between someone with superior power and someone who is without power and helpless—which may afford a transition to the hypnosis of fright which occurs in animals. The manner in which it is produced and its relationship to sleep are not clear; and the puzzling way in which some people are subject to it, while others resist it completely, points to some factor still unknown which is realized in it and which perhaps alone makes possible the purity of the attitudes of the libido which it exhibits. It is noticeable that, even when there is complete suggestive compliance in other respects, the moral conscience of the person hypnotized may show resistance. But this may be due to the fact that in hypnosis as it is usually practiced some knowledge may be retained that what is happening is only a game, an untrue reproduction of another situation of far more importance to life.

But after the preceding discussions we are quite in a position to give the formula for the libidinal constitution of groups, or at least of such groups as we have hitherto considered—namely, those that have a leader and have not been able by means of too much "organization" to acquire secondarily the characteristics of an individual. *A primary group of this kind is a number of individuals who have put one and the same object in the place of their ego ideal and have consequently identified themselves with one another in their ego.* This condition admits of graphic representation:

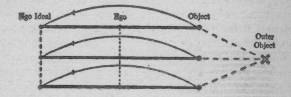

# IX

## THE HERD INSTINCT

WE cannot for long enjoy the illusion that we have solved the riddle of the group with this formula. It is impossible to escape the immediate and disturbing recollection that all we have really done has been to shift the question on to the riddle of hypnosis, about which so many points have yet to be cleared up. And now another objection shows us our further path.

It might be said that the intense emotional ties which we observe in groups are quite sufficient to explain one of their characteristics—the lack of independence and initiative in their members, the similarity in the reactions of all of them, their reduction, so to speak, to the level of group individuals. But if we look at it as a whole, a group shows us more than this. Some of its features—the weakness of intellectual ability, the lack of emotional restraint, the incapacity for moderation and delay, the inclination to exceed every limit in the expression of emotion and to work it off completely in the form of action—these and similar features, which we find so impressively described in Le Bon, show an unmistakable picture of a regression of mental activity to an earlier stage such as we are not surprised to find among savages or children. A regression of this sort is in particular an essential characteristic of common groups, while, as we have heard, in organized and artificial groups it can to a large extent be checked.

We thus have an impression of a state in which an individual's private emotional impulses and intellectual acts are too weak to come to anything by themselves and are entirely dependent for this on being reinforced by being repeated in a similar way in the other members of the group. We are reminded of how many of these phenomena of dependence are part of the normal constitution of human society, of how little originality and personal courage are to be found in it, of how much every individual is ruled by those attitudes of the group mind which exhibit themselves in such forms as racial characteristics, class prejudices, public opinion, etc. The influence of suggestion becomes a greater riddle for us when we admit that it is not exercised only by the leader, but by every individual upon every other individual; and we must reproach ourselves with having unfairly emphasized the relation to the leader and with having kept the other factor of mutual suggestion too much in the background.

After this encouragement to modesty, we shall be inclined to another voice, which promises us an explanation based upon simpler grounds. Such a one is to be found in Trotter's thoughtful book on the herd instinct (1916), concerning which my only regret is that it does not entirely escape the antipathies that were set loose by the recent great war.

Trotter derives the mental phenomena that are described as occurring in groups from a herd instinct ("gregariousness"[1]), which is innate in human beings just as in other species of animals. Biologically, he says, this gregariousness is an analogy to multicellularity and as it were a continuation of it. (In terms of the libido theory it is a further manifestation of the tendency which proceeds from the libido and which is felt by all living beings of the same kind, to combine

---

1 [This word is in English in the original.]

in more and more comprehensive units.[1]) The individual feels incomplete if he is alone. The fear shown by small children would seem already to be an expression of this herd instinct. Opposition to the herd is as good as separation from it, and is therefore anxiously avoided. But the herd turns away from anything that is new or unusual. The herd instinct would appear to be something primary, something which cannot be split up.[2]

Trotter gives as the list of instincts which he considers as primary those of self-preservation, of nutrition, of sex, and of the herd. The last often comes into opposition with the others. The feelings of guilt and of duty are the peculiar possessions of a gregarious animal. Trotter also derives from the herd instinct the repressive forces which psychoanalysis has shown to exist in the ego, and from the same source accordingly the resistances which the physician comes up against in psychoanalytic treatment. Speech owes its importance to its aptitude for mutual understanding in the herd, and upon it the identification of the individuals with one another largely rests.

While Le Bon is principally concerned with typical transient group formations, and McDougall with stable associations, Trotter has chosen as the center of his interest the most generalized form of assemblage in which man, that ζῷον πολιτικόν,[3] passes his life, and he gives us its psychological basis. But Trotter is under no necessity of tracing back the herd instinct, for he characterizes it as primary and not further reducible. Boris Sidis's attempt, to which he refers, at tracing the herd instinct back to suggestibility is fortunately superfluous as far as he is concerned; it is an explanation of a familiar and unsatisfactory type, and the converse proposition—that suggestibility is a derivative of the

---

[1] See *Beyond the Pleasure Principle* (1920).
[2] [The last five words are in English in the original.]
[3] ["Political animal" (Aristotle, *Politics*).]

herd instinct—would seem to me to throw far more light on the subject.

But Trotter's exposition is open, with even more justice than the others, to the objection that it takes too little account of the leader's part in a group, while we incline rather to the opposite judgment, that it is impossible to grasp the nature of a group if the leader is disregarded. The herd instinct leaves no room at all for the leader; he is merely thrown in along with the herd, almost by chance; it follows, too, that no path leads from this instinct to the need for a God; the herd is without a herdsman. But besides this, Trotter's exposition can be undermined psychologically; that is to say, it can be made at all events probable that the herd instinct is not irreducible, that it is not primary in the same sense as the instinct of self-preservation and the sexual instinct.

It is naturally no easy matter to trace the ontogenesis of the herd instinct. The fear which is shown by small children when they are left alone, and which Trotter claims as being already a manifestation of the instinct, nevertheless suggests more readily another interpretation. The fear relates to the child's mother, and later to other familiar people, and it is the expression of an unfulfilled desire, which the child does not yet know how to deal with in any way except by turning it into anxiety.[1] Nor is the child's fear when it is alone pacified by the sight of any haphazard "member of the herd," but on the contrary it is brought into existence by the approach of a "stranger" of this sort. Then for a long time nothing in the nature of herd instinct or group feeling is to be observed in children. Something like it first grows up, in a nursery containing many children, out of the children's relation to their parents, and it does so as a reaction to the initial

---

[1] See the remarks upon anxiety in my *Introductory Lectures* (1916–17), Lecture XXV.

envy with which the elder child receives the younger one. The elder child would certainly like to put his successor jealously aside, to keep it away from the parents, and to rob it of all its privileges; but in the face of the fact that this younger child (like all that come later) is loved by the parents as much as he himself is, and in consequence of the impossibility of his maintaining his hostile attitude without damaging himself, he is forced into identifying himself with the other children. So there grows up in the troop of children a communal or group feeling, which is then further developed at school. The first demand made by this reaction-formation is for justice, for equal treatment for all. We all know how loudly and implacably this claim is put forward at school. If one cannot be the favorite oneself, at all events nobody else shall be the favorite. This transformation—the replacing of jealousy by a group feeling in the nursery and classroom—might be considered improbable, if the same process could not later on be observed again in other circumstances. We have only to think of the troop of women and girls, all of them in love in an enthusiastically sentimental way, who crowd round a singer or pianist after his performance. It would certainly be easy for each of them to be jealous of the rest; but, in the face of their numbers and the consequent impossibility of their reaching the aim of their love, they renounce it, and, instead of pulling out one another's hair, they act as a united group, do homage to the hero of the occasion with their common actions, and would probably be glad to have a share of *his* flowing locks. Originally rivals, they have succeeded in identifying themselves with one another by means of a similar love for the same object. When, as is usual, an instinctual situation is capable of various outcomes, we shall not be surprised that the actual outcome is one which brings with it the possibility of a certain amount of satisfaction, whereas some other outcome, in itself more obvious, is passed over because the circumstances of life prevent its leading to any such satisfaction.

What appears later on in society in the shape of *Gemeingeist, esprit de corps*, "group spirit," etc., does not belie its derivation from what was originally envy. No one must want to put himself forward, every one must be the same and have the same. Social justice means that we deny ourselves many things so that others may have to do without them as well, or, what is the same thing, may not be able to ask for them. This demand for equality is the root of social conscience and the sense of duty. It reveals itself unexpectedly in the syphilitic's dread of infecting other people, which psychoanalysis has taught us to understand. The dread exhibited by these poor wretches corresponds to their violent struggles against the unconscious wish to spread their infection on to other people; for why should they alone be infected and cut off from so much? why not other people as well? And the same germ is to be found in the apt story of the judgment of Solomon. If one woman's child is dead, the other shall not have a live one either. The bereaved woman is recognized by this wish.

Thus social feeling is based upon the reversal of what was first a hostile feeling into a positively-toned tie in the nature of an identification. So far as we have hitherto been able to follow the course of events, this reversal seems to occur under the influence of a common affectionate tie with a person outside the group. We do not ourselves regard our analysis of identification as exhaustive, but it is enough for our present purpose that we should revert to this one feature—its demand that equalization shall be consistently carried through. We have already heard in the discussion of the two artificial groups, Church and army, that their necessary precondition is that all their members should be loved in the same way by one person, the leader. Do not let us forget, however, that the demand for equality in a group applies only to its members and not to the leader. All the members must be equal to one another, but they all want to be ruled by one person. Many equals, who can identify themselves with one another, and a single person superior to them all—that is the situation that we find realized in groups which are capable of subsisting. Let us venture, then, to correct Trotter's pronouncement that man is a herd animal and assert that he is rather a horde animal, an individual creature in a horde led by a chief.

# X

# THE GROUP AND THE PRIMAL HORDE

IN 1912 I took up a conjecture of Darwin's to the effect that the primitive form of human society was that of a horde ruled over despotically by a powerful male. I attempted to show that the fortunes of this horde have left indestructible traces upon the history of human descent; and, especially, that the development of totemism, which comprises in itself the beginnings of religion, morality, and social organization, is connected with the killing of the chief by violence and the transformation of the paternal horde into a community of brothers.[1] To be sure, this is only a hypothesis, like so many others with which archaeologists endeavor to lighten the darkness of prehistoric times—a "Just-So-Story," as it was amusingly called by a not unkind English critic;[2] but I think it is creditable to such a hypothesis if it proves able to bring coherence and understanding into more and more new regions.

Human groups exhibit once again the familiar picture of an individual of superior strength among a troop of equal companions, a picture which is also contained in our idea of the primal horde. The psy-

[1] *Totem and Taboo* (1912–13) [Essay IV. Freud uses the term "horde" to signify a relatively small collection of people.]

[2] [In the 1st edition only, the name "Kroeger" appeared here. This was evidently a misprint for "Kroeber"—incidentally the name of the well-known *American* anthropologist. But see the addendum on p. 77.]

chology of such a group, as we know it from the
descriptions to which we have so often referred—the
dwindling of the conscious individual personality, the
focusing of thoughts and feelings into a common direction, the predominance of the affective side of the
mind and of unconscious psychical life, the tendency
to the immediate carrying out of intentions as they
emerge—all this corresponds to a state of regression to
a primitive mental activity, of just such a sort as we
should be inclined to ascribe to the primal horde.[1]

Thus the group appears to us as a revival of the
primal horde. Just as primitive man survives poten-
tially in every individual, so the primal horde may
arise once more out of any random collection; in so far
as men are habitually under the sway of group formation we recognize in it the survival of the primal horde.
We must conclude that the psychology of groups is
the oldest human psychology; what we have isolated as
individual psychology, by neglecting all traces of the
group, has once since come into prominence out of the
old group psychology, by a gradual process which may
still, perhaps, be described as incomplete. We shall

[1] What we have just described in our general characterization
of mankind must apply especially to the primal horde. The will
of the individual was too weak; if he did not venture upon
action. No impulses whatever came into existence except collective ones; there was only a common will, there were no single
ones. An idea did not dare to turn itself into an act of will un-
less it felt itself reinforced by a perception of its general diffu-
sion. This weakness of the idea is to be explained by the strength
of the emotional tie which is shared by all the members of the
horde; but the similarity in the circumstances of their life and
the absence of any private property assist in determining the
uniformity of their individual mental acts. As we may observe
with children and soldiers, common activity is not excluded
even in the excretory functions. The one great exception is
provided by the sexual act, in which a third person is at best
superfluous and in the extreme case is condemned to a state of
painful expectancy. As to the reaction of the sexual need (for
genital satisfaction) toward gregariousness, see below [p. 93].

later venture upon an attempt at specifying the point of departure of this development. [See p. 86 ff.]

Further reflection will show us in what respect this statement requires correction. Individual psychology must, on the contrary, be just as old as group psychology, for from the first there were two kinds of psychologies, that of the individual members of the group and that of the father, chief, or leader. The members of the group were subject to ties just as we see them today, but the father of the primal horde was free. His intellectual acts were strong and independent even in isolation, and his will needed no reinforcement from others. Consistency leads us to assume that his ego had few libidinal ties; he loved no one but himself, or other people only in so far as they served his needs. To objects his ego gave away no more than was barely necessary.

He, at the very beginning of the history of mankind, was the "superman" whom Nietzsche only expected from the future. Even today the members of a group stand in need of the illusion that they are equally and justly loved by their leader; but the leader himself need love no one else, he may be of a masterful nature, absolutely narcissistic, self-confident and independent. We know that love puts a check upon narcissism, and it would be possible to show how, by operating in this way, it became a factor of civilization.

The primal father of the horde was not yet immortal, as he later became by deification. If he died, he had to be replaced; his place was probably taken by a youngest son, who had up to then been a member of the group like any other. There must therefore be a possibility of transforming group psychology into individual psychology; a condition must be discovered under which such a transformation is easily accomplished, just as it is possible for bees in case of necessity to turn a larva into a queen instead of into a worker. One can imagine only one possibility: the primal father had prevented his sons from satisfying their directly sexual impulsions; he forced them into abstinence and consequently into the emotional ties with him and with one another which could arise out of those of their impulsions that were inhibited in their sexual aim. He forced them, so to speak, into group psychology. His sexual jealousy and intolerance became in the last resort the causes of group psychology.[1]

Whoever became his successor was also given the possibility of sexual satisfaction, and was by that means offered a way out of the conditions of group psychology. The fixation of the libido to women and the possibility of satisfaction without any need for delay or accumulation made an end of the importance of those of his sexual impulsions that were inhibited in their aim, and allowed his narcissism always to rise to its full height. We shall return in a postscript [p. 89 ff.] to this connection between love and character formation.

We may further emphasize, as being specially instructive, the relation that holds between the contrivance by means of which an artificial group is held together and the constitution of the primal horde. We have seen that with an army and a Church this contrivance is the illusion that the leader loves all of the individuals equally and justly. But this is simply an idealistic remodeling of the state of affairs in the primal horde, where all of the sons knew that they were equally *persecuted* by the primal father, and *feared* him equally. This same recasting upon which

[1] It may perhaps also be assumed that the sons, when they were driven out and separated from their father, advanced from identification with one another to homosexual object-love, and in this way won freedom to kill their father. [See *Totem and Taboo, Standard Ed.*, 13, 144.]

all social duties are built up is already presupposed
by the next form of human society, the totemic clan.
The indestructible strength of the family as a natural
group formation rests upon the fact that this necessary presupposition of the father's equal love can have
a real application in the family.

But we expect even more of this derivation of the
group from the primal horde. It ought also to help
us to understand what is still incomprehensible and
mysterious in group formations—all that lies hidden
behind the enigmatic words "hypnosis" and "suggestion." And I think it can succeed in this too. Let us
recall that hypnosis has something positively uncanny
about it; but the characteristic of uncanniness suggests
something old and familiar that has undergone repression.[1] Let us consider how hypnosis is induced. The
hypnotist asserts that he is in possession of a mysterious
power that robs the subject of his own will; or, which
is the same thing, the subject believes it of him. This
mysterious power (which is even now often described
popularly as "animal magnetism") must be the same
power that is looked upon by primitive people as the
source of taboo, the same that emanates from kings and
chieftains and makes it dangerous to approach them
(*mana*). The hypnotist, then, is supposed to be in
possession of this power; and how does he manifest it?
By telling the subject to look him in the eyes; his most
typical method of hypnotizing is by his look. But it is
precisely the *sight* of the chieftain that is dangerous
and unbearable for primitive people, just as later that
of the Godhead is for mortals. Even Moses had to act
as an intermediary between his people and Jehovah,
since the people could not support the sight of God;
and when he returned from the presence of God his
face shone—some of the *mana* had been transferred on

[1] Cf. "The 'Uncanny'" (1919).

to him, just as happens with the intermediary among primitive people.[1]

It is true that hypnosis can also be evoked in other ways, for instance by fixing the eyes upon a bright object or by listening to a monotonous sound. This is misleading and has given occasion to inadequate physiological theories. In point of fact these procedures merely serve to divert conscious attention and to hold it riveted. The situation is the same as if the hypnotist had said to the subject: "Now concern yourself exclusively with my person; the rest of the world is quite uninteresting." It would of course be technically inexpedient for a hypnotist to make such a speech; it would tear the subject away from his unconscious attitude and stimulate him to conscious opposition. The hypnotist avoids directing the subject's conscious thoughts toward his own intentions, and makes the person upon whom he is experimenting sink into an activity in which the world is bound to seem uninteresting to him; but at the same time the subject is in reality unconsciously concentrating his whole attention upon the hypnotist, and is getting into an attitude of *rapport*, of transference on to him. Thus the indirect methods of hypnotizing, like many of the technical procedures used in making jokes,[2] have the effect of checking certain distributions of mental energy which would interfere with the course of events in the unconscious, and they lead eventually to the same result as

[1] See *Totem and Taboo* [second essay] and the sources there quoted.

[2] [The distracting of attention as part of the technique of joking is discussed at some length in the latter half of Chapter V of Freud's book on jokes (1905). The possibility of this mechanism playing a part in "thought-transference" is mentioned in *Psycho-Analysis and Telepathy* (1921) *Standard Ed.*, 18, 175. But perhaps Freud's earliest allusion to the idea is to be found in his final chapter in *Studies on Hysteria* (Breuer and Freud, 1895). Toward the beginning of the second section of that chapter Freud brings forward this same mechanism as a possible part explanation of the efficacy of his "pressure" procedure.]

the direct methods of influence by means of staring or stroking.[1]

Ferenczi [1909] has made the true discovery that when a hypnotist gives the command to sleep, which is often done at the beginning of hypnosis, he is putting himself in the place of the subject's parents. He thinks that two sorts of hypnotism are to be distinguished: one coaxing and soothing, which he considers is modeled on the mother, and another threatening, which is derived from the father. Now the command to sleep in hypnosis means nothing more nor less than an order to withdraw all interest from the world and to concentrate it on the person of the hypnotist. And it is so understood by the subject; for in this withdrawal of interest from the external world lies the psychological characteristic of sleep, and the kinship between sleep and the state of hypnosis is based on it.

By the measures that he takes, then, the hypnotist awakens in the subject a portion of his archaic heritage which had also made him compliant toward his parents and which had experienced an individual re-animation in his relation to his father; what is thus awakened is the idea of a paramount and dangerous

1 This situation, in which the subject's attitude is unconsciously directed toward the hypnotist, while he is consciously occupied with monotonous and uninteresting perceptions, finds a parallel among the events of psychoanalytic treatment, which deserves to be mentioned here. At least once in the course of every analysis a moment comes when the patient obstinately maintains that just now positively nothing whatever occurs to his mind. His free associations come to a stop and the usual incentives for putting them in motion fail in their effect. If the analyst insists, the patient is at last induced to admit that he is thinking of the view from the consulting-room window, of the wallpaper that he sees before him, or of the gas-lamp hanging from the ceiling. Then one knows at once that he has gone off into the transference and that he is engaged upon what are still unconscious thoughts relating to the physician; and one sees the stoppage in the patient's associations disappear, as soon as he has been given this explanation.

personality, toward whom only a passive-masochistic attitude is possible, to whom one's will has to be surrendered,—while to be alone with him, "to look him in the face," appears a hazardous enterprise. It is only in some such way as this that we can picture the relation of the individual member of the primal horde to the primal father. As we know from other reactions, individuals have preserved a variable degree of personal aptitude for reviving old situations of this kind. Some knowledge that in spite of everything hypnosis is only a game, a deceptive renewal of these old impressions, may, however, remain behind and take care that there is a resistance against any too serious consequences of the suspension of the will in hypnosis.

The uncanny and coercive characteristics of group formations, which are shown in the phenomena of suggestion that accompany them, may therefore with justice be traced back to the fact of their origin from the primal horde. The leader of the group is still the dreaded primal father; the group still wishes to be governed by unrestricted force; it has an extreme passion for authority; in Le Bon's phrase, it has a thirst for obedience. The primal father is the group ideal, which governs the ego in the place of the ego ideal. Hypnosis has a good claim to being described as a group of two. There remains as a definition for suggestion: a conviction which is not based upon perception and reasoning but upon an erotic tie.[1]

[1] It seems to me worth emphasizing the fact that the discussions in this section have induced us to give up Bernheim's conception of hypnosis and go back to the *naïf* earlier one. According to Bernheim all hypnotic phenomena are to be traced to the factor of suggestion, which is not itself capable of further explanation. We have come to the conclusion that suggestion is a partial manifestation of the state of hypnosis, and that hypnosis is solidly founded upon a predisposition which has survived in the unconscious from the early history of the human family. [Freud had already expressed his skepticism about Bernheim's views on suggestion in the preface to his translation of Bernheim's book on the subject (1888–9).]

[*Addendum to footnote* 2, p. 69:—Kroeber's original review of *Totem and Taboo,* published in *Amer. Anthropol.,* New Series, 22 (1920), 48, contained no reference to a "just-so story." This was pointed out by Kroeber himself in a second review, published nearly twenty years later in *Amer. J. Sociol.* 45, (1939), 446. The comparison with a "just-so story" was actually made in a review of *Totem and Taboo* by the English anthropologist R. R. Marett in *The Athenaeum,* Feb. 13, 1920, p. 206.]

# A DIFFERENTIATING GRADE IN THE EGO

IF we survey the life of an individual man of today,
bearing in mind the mutually complementary accounts
of group psychology given by the authorities, we may
lose the courage, in face of the complications that are
revealed, to attempt a comprehensive exposition. Each
individual is a component part of numerous groups,
he is bound by ties of identification in many directions, and he has built up his ego ideal upon the most
various models. Each individual therefore has a share
in numerous group minds—those of his race, of his
class, of his creed, of his nationality, etc.—and he can
also raise himself above them to the extent of having
a scrap of independence and originality. Such stable
and lasting group formations, with their uniform and
constant effects, are less striking to an observer than
the rapidly formed and transient groups from which
Le Bon has made his brilliant psychological character
sketch of the group mind. And it is just in these noisy
ephemeral groups, which are as it were superimposed
upon the others, that we are met by the prodigy of the
complete, even though only temporary, disappearance
of exactly what we have recognized as individual
acquirements.

We have interpreted this prodigy as meaning that
the individual gives up his ego ideal and substitutes
for it the group ideal as embodied in the leader. And
we must add by way of correction that the prodigy is

not equally great in every case. In many individuals
the separation between the ego and the ego ideal is not
very far advanced; the two still coincide readily; the
ego has often preserved its earlier narcissistic self-
complacency. The selection of the leader is very much
facilitated by this circumstance. He need often only
possess the typical qualities of the individuals concerned in a particularly clearly marked and pure form,
and need only give an impression of greater force and
of more freedom of libido; and in that case the need
for a strong chief will often meet him half-way and
invest him with a predominance to which he would
otherwise perhaps have had no claim. The other members of the group, whose ego ideal would not, apart
from this, have become embodied in his person without some correction, are then carried away with the
rest by "suggestion," that is to say, by means of
identification.

We are aware that what we have been able to con-
tribute toward the explanation of the libidinal structure of groups leads back to the distinction between
the ego and the ego ideal and to the double kind of tie
which this makes possible—identification, and putting
the object in the place of the ego ideal. The assumption of this kind of differentiating grade in the ego as
a first step in analysis of the ego must gradually establish its justification in the most various regions of
psychology. In my paper on narcissism [1914] I have
put together all the pathological material that could
at the moment be used in support of this differentiation. But it may be expected that when we penetrate
deeper into the psychology of the psychoses its significance will be discovered to be far greater. Let us
reflect that the ego now enters into the relation of an
object to the ego ideal which has been developed out
of it, and that all the interplay between an external
object and the ego as a whole, with which our study
of the neuroses has made us acquainted, may possibly

be repeated upon this new scene of action within the ego.

In this place I shall only follow up one of the consequences which seem possible from this point of view, thus resuming the discussion of a problem which I was obliged to leave unsolved elsewhere.[1] Each of the mental differentiations that we have become acquainted with represents a fresh aggravation of the difficulties of mental functioning, increases its instability, and may become the starting-point for its breakdown, that is, for the onset of a disease. Thus, by being born we have made the step from an absolutely self-sufficient narcissism to the perception of a changing external world and the beginnings of the discovery of objects. And with this is associated the fact that we cannot endure the new state of things for long, that we periodically revert from it, in our sleep, to our former condition of absence of stimulation and avoidance of objects. It is true, however, that in this we are following a hint from the external world, which, by means of the periodical change of day and night, temporarily withdraws the greater part of the stimuli that affect us. The second example of such a step, pathologically more important, is subject to no such qualification. In the course of our development we have effected a separation of our mental existence into a coherent ego and into an unconscious and repressed portion which is left outside it; and we know that the stability of this new acquisition is exposed to constant shocks. In dreams and in neuroses which is thus excluded knocks for admission at the gates, guarded though they are by resistances; and in our waking health we make use of special artifices for allowing what is repressed to circumvent the resistances and for receiving it temporarily into our ego to the increase of our pleasure. Jokes and humor, and to some extent the comic in general, may be regarded in

[1] "Mourning and Melancholia" (1917).

this light. Everyone acquainted with the psychology of the neuroses will think of similar examples of less importance; but I hasten on to the application I have in view.

It is quite conceivable that the separation of the ego ideal from the ego cannot be borne for long either, and has to be temporarily undone. In all renunciations and limitations imposed upon the ego a periodical infringement of the prohibition is the rule; this indeed is shown by the institution of festivals, which in origin are nothing less nor more than excesses provided by law and which owe their cheerful character to the release which they bring.[1] The Saturnalia of the Romans and our modern carnival agree in this essential feature with the festivals of primitive people, which usually end in debaucheries of every kind and the transgression of what are at other times the most sacred commandments. But the ego ideal comprises the sum of all the limitations in which the ego has to acquiesce, and for that reason the abrogation of the ideal would necessarily be a magnificent festival for the ego, which might then once again feel satisfied with itself.[2]

There is always a feeling of triumph when something in the ego coincides with the ego ideal. And the sense of guilt (as well as the sense of inferiority) can also be understood as an expression of tension between the ego and the ego ideal.

It is well known that there are people the general color of whose mood oscillates periodically from an excessive depression through some kind of intermediate state to an exalted sense of well-being. These oscillations appear in very different degrees of amplitude,

---

[1] *Totem and Taboo* [*Standard Ed.*, 13, 140].
[2] Trotter traces repression back to the herd instinct. It is a translation of this into another form of expression rather than a contradiction when I say in my paper on narcissism [1914, near the beginning of Part III] that "for the ego the formation of an ideal would be the conditioning factor of repression."

from what is just noticeable to those extreme instances which, in the shape of melancholia and mania, make the most tormenting or disturbing inroads upon the life of the person concerned. In typical cases of this cyclical depression external precipitating causes do not seem to play any decisive part; as regards internal motives, nothing more, or nothing else is to be found in these patients than in all others. It has consequently become the custom to consider these cases as not being psychogenic. We shall refer presently to those other exactly similar cases of cyclical depression which *can* easily be traced back to mental traumas.

Thus the foundation of these spontaneous oscillations of mood is unknown; we are without insight into the mechanism of the displacement of a melancholia by a mania. So we are free to suppose that these patients are people in whom our conjecture might find an actual application—their ego ideal might be temporarily resolved into their ego after having previously ruled it with especial strictness.

Let us keep to what is clear: On the basis of our analysis of the ego it cannot be doubted that in cases of mania the ego and the ego ideal have fused together, so that the person, in a mood of triumph and self-satisfaction, disturbed by no self-criticism, can enjoy the abolition of his inhibitions, his feelings of consideration for others, and his self-reproaches. It is not so obvious, but nevertheless very probable, that the misery of the melancholic is the expression of a sharp conflict between the two agencies of his ego, a conflict in which the ideal, in an excess of sensitiveness, relentlessly exhibits its condemnation of the ego in delusions of inferiority and in self-depreciation. The only question is whether we are to look for the causes of these altered relations between the ego and the ego ideal in the periodic rebellions, which we have postulated above, against the new institution, or whether we are to make other circumstances responsible for them.

A change into mania is not an indispensable feature of the symptomatology of melancholic depression. There are simple melancholias, some in single and some in recurrent attacks, which never show this development.

On the other hand there are melancholias in which the precipitating cause clearly plays an etiological part. They are those which occur after the loss of a loved object, whether by death or as the result of circumstances which have necessitated the withdrawal of the libido from the object. A psychogenic melancholia of this sort can end in mania, and this cycle can be repeated several times, just as easily as in a case which appears to be spontaneous. Thus the state of things is somewhat obscure, especially as only a few forms and cases of melancholia have been submitted to psychoanalytic investigation.[1] So far we only understand those cases in which the object is given up because it has shown itself unworthy of love. It is then set up again inside the ego, by means of identification, and severely condemned by the ego ideal. The reproaches and attacks directed toward the object come to light in the shape of melancholic self-reproaches.[2]

A melancholia of this kind, too, may end in a change into mania; so that the possibility of this happening represents a feature which is independent of the other characteristics of the clinical picture.

Nevertheless I see no difficulty in assigning to the factor of the periodic rebellion of the ego against the ego ideal a share in both kinds of melancholia, the psychogenic as well as the spontaneous. In the spontaneous kind it may be supposed that the ego ideal is inclined to display a peculiar strictness, which then

[1] Cf. Abraham (1912).
[2] To speak more accurately, they conceal themselves behind the reproaches directed toward the subject's own ego, and lend them the fixity, tenacity, and imperativeness which characterize the self-reproaches of a melancholic.

results automatically in its temporary suspension. In the psychogenic kind the ego would be incited to rebellion by ill-treatment on the part of its ideal— an ill-treatment which it encounters when there has been identification with a rejected object.[1]

---

[1] [Some further discussion of melancholia will be found in Chapter V of *The Ego and the Id* (1923).]

# XII

## POSTSCRIPT

In the course of the inquiry which has just been
brought to a provisional end we came across a number
of side-paths which we avoided pursuing in the first
instance but in which there was much that offered us
promises of insight. We propose now to take up a few
of the points that have been left on one side in this
way.

A. The distinction between identification of the ego
with an object and replacement of the ego ideal by an
object finds an interesting illustration in the two great
artificial groups which we began by studying, the army
and the Christian Church.

It is obvious that a soldier takes his superior, that is,
in fact, the leader of the army, as his ideal, while he
identifies himself with his equals, and derives from
this community of their egos the obligations for giving
mutual help and for sharing possessions which com-
radeship implies. But he becomes ridiculous if he tries
to identify himself with the general. The soldier in
*Wallensteins Lager* laughs at the sergeant for this very
reason:

> Wie er räuspert und wie er spuckt,
> Das habt ihr ihm glücklich abgeguckt![1]

[1] [I grant you, your counterfeit perfectly fits
  The way that he hawks and the way that he spits.
                    (Scene 6 of Schiller's play.)]

It is otherwise in the Catholic Church. Every Christian loves Christ as his ideal and feels himself united with all other Christians by the tie of identification. But the Church requires more of him. He has also to identify himself with Christ and love all other Christians as Christ loved them. At both points, therefore, the Church requires that the position of the libido which is given by group formation should be supplemented. Identification has to be added where object-choice has taken place, and object-love where there is identification. This addition evidently goes beyond the constitution of the group. One can be a good Christian and yet be far from the idea of putting oneself in Christ's place and of having like him an all-embracing love for mankind. One need not think oneself capable, weak mortal that one is, of the Savior's largeness of soul and strength of love. But this further development in the distribution of libido in the group is probably the factor upon which Christianity bases its claim to have reached a higher ethical level.

B. We have said that it would be possible to specify the point in the mental development of mankind at which the advance from group psychology to individual psychology was achieved also by the individual members of the group [p. 71].[1]

For this purpose we must return for a moment to the scientific myth of the father of the primal horde. He was later on exalted into the creator of the world, and with justice, for he had produced all the sons who composed the first group. He was the ideal of each one of them, at once feared and honored, a fact which led later to the idea of taboo. These many individuals

[1] What follows at this point was written under the influence of an exchange of ideas with Otto Rank. [*Added* 1923:] See also Rank (1922). [This passage is to be read in conjunction with Sections 5, 6 and 7 of the fourth essay in *Totem and Taboo, Standard Ed.*, 13, 140 ff.]

eventually banded themselves together, killed him and cut him in pieces. None of the group of victors could take his place, or, if one of them did, the battles began afresh, until they understood that they must all renounce their father's heritage. They then formed the totemic community of brothers, all with equal rights and united by the totem prohibitions which were to preserve and to expiate the memory of the murder. But the dissatisfaction with what had been achieved still remained, and it became the source of new developments. The persons who were united in this group of brothers gradually came toward a revival of the old state of things at a new level. The male became once more the chief of a family, and broke down the prerogatives of the gynaecocracy which had become established during the fatherless period. As a compensation for this he may at that time have acknowledged the mother deities, whose priests were castrated for the mother's protection, after the example that had been given by the father of the primal horde. And yet the new family was only a shadow of the old one; there were numbers of fathers and each one was limited by the rights of the others.

It was then, perhaps, that some individual, in the exigency of his longing, may have been moved to free himself from the group and take over the father's part. He who did this was the first epic poet; and the advance was achieved in his imagination. This poet disguised the truth with lies in accordance with his longing. He invented the heroic myth. The hero was a man who by himself had slain the father—the father who still appeared in the myth as a totemic monster. Just as the father had been the boy's first ideal, so in the hero who aspires to the father's place the poet now created the first ego ideal. The transition to the hero was probably afforded by the youngest son, the mother's favorite, whom she had protected from paternal jealousy, and who, in the era of the primal horde, had been the father's successor. In the lying poetic fancies of prehistoric times the woman, who had been the prize of battle and the temptation to murder, was probably turned into the active seducer and instigator to the crime.

The hero claims to have acted alone in accomplishing the deed, which certainly only the horde as a whole would have ventured upon. But, as Rank has observed, fairy tales have preserved clear traces of the facts which were disavowed. For we often find in them that the hero who has to carry out some difficult task (usually the youngest son, and not infrequently one who has represented himself to the father-substitute as being stupid, that is to say, harmless)—we often find, then, that this hero can carry out his task only by the help of a crowd of small animals, such as bees or ants. These would be the brothers in the primal horde, just as in the same way in dream symbolism insects or vermin signify brothers and sisters (contemptuously, considered as babies). Moreover every one of the tasks in myths and fairy tales is easily recognizable as a substitute for the heroic deed.

The myth, then, is the step by which the individual emerges from group psychology. The first myth was certainly the psychological, the hero myth; the explanatory nature myth must have followed much later. The poet who had taken this step and had in this way set himself free from the group in his imagination, is nevertheless able (as Rank has further observed) to find his way back to it in reality. For he goes and relates to the group his hero's deeds which he has invented. At bottom this hero is no one but himself. Thus he lowers himself to the level of reality, and raises his hearers to the level of imagination. But his hearers understand the poet, and, in virtue of their having the same relation of longing toward the primal father, they can identify themselves with the hero.[1]

1 Cf. Hanns Sachs (1920).

The lie of the heroic myth culminates in the deification of the hero. Perhaps the deified hero may have been earlier than the Father God and may have been a precursor to the return of the primal father as a deity. The series of gods, then, would run chronologically: Mother Goddess—Hero—Father God. But it is only with the elevation of the never-forgotten primal father that the deity acquires the features that we still recognize in him today.[1]

C. A great deal has been said in this paper about directly sexual instincts and those that are inhibited in their aims, and it may be hoped that this distinction will not meet with too much resistance. But a detailed discussion of the question will not be out of place, even if it only repeats what has to a great extent already been said before.

The development of the libido in children has made us acquainted with the first but also the best example of sexual instincts which are inhibited in their aims. All the feelings which a child has toward its parents and those who look after it pass by an easy transition into the wishes which give expression to the child's sexual impulses. The child claims from these objects of its love all the signs of affection which it knows of; it wants to kiss them, touch them, and look at them; it is curious to see their genitals, and to be with them when they perform their intimate excretory functions; it promises to marry its mother or nurse—whatever it may understand by marriage; it proposes to itself to bear its father a child, etc. Direct observation, as well as the subsequent analytic investigation of the residues of childhood, leave no doubt as to the complete fusion of tender and jealous feelings and of sexual intentions,

---

[1] In this brief exposition I have made no attempt to bring forward any of the material existing in legends, myths, fairy tales, the history of manners, etc., in support of the construction.

and show us in what a fundamental way the child
makes the person it loves into the object of all its still
not properly centered sexual trends.[1]

This first configuration of the child's love, which in
typical cases takes the shape of the Oedipus complex,
succumbs, as we know, from the beginning of the
period of latency onward to a wave of repression.
Such of it as is left over shows itself as a purely affectionate emotional tie, relating to the same people, but
no longer to be described as "sexual." Psychoanalysis,
which illuminates the depths of mental life, has no
difficulty in showing that the sexual ties of the earliest
years of childhood also persist, though repressed and
unconscious. It gives us courage to assert that wherever we come across an affectionate feeling it is successor to a completely "sensual" object-tie with the
person in question or rather with that person's proto-
type (or *imago*). It cannot indeed disclose to us without a special investigation whether in a given case
this former complete sexual current still exists under
repression or whether it has already been exhausted.
To speak still more precisely: it is quite certain that
this current is still there as a form and possibility, and
can always be cathected and put into activity again by
means of regression; the only question is (and it cannot always be answered) what degree of cathexis and
operative force it still has at the present moment.
Equal care must be taken in this connection to avoid
two sources of error—the Scylla of underestimating
the importance of the repressed unconscious, and the
Charybdis of judging the normal entirely by the standards of the pathological.

A psychology which will not or cannot penetrate
the depths of what is repressed regards affectionate
emotional ties as being invariably the expression of
impulsions which have no sexual aim, even though

[1] Cf. my *Three Essays* (1905) [*Standard Ed.,* 7, 199].

they are derived from impulsions which have such an aim.[1]

We are justified in saying that they have been diverted from these sexual aims, even though there is some difficulty in giving a description of such a diversion of aim which will conform to the requirements of metapsychology. Moreover, those instincts which are inhibited in their aims always preserve some few of their original sexual aims; even an affectionate devotee, even a friend or an admirer, desires the physical proximity and the sight of the person who is now loved only in the "Pauline" sense. If we choose, we may recognize in this diversion of aim a beginning of the *sublimation* of the sexual instincts, or on the other hand we may fix the limits of sublimation at some more distant point. Those sexual instincts which are inhibited in their aims have a great functional advantage over those which are uninhibited. Since they are not capable of really complete satisfaction, they are especially adapted to create permanent ties; while those instincts which are directly sexual incur a loss of energy each time they are satisfied, and must wait to be renewed by a fresh accumulation of sexual libido, so that meanwhile the object may have been changed. The inhibited instincts are capable of any degree of admixture with the uninhibited; they can be transformed back into them, just as they arose out of them. It is well known how easily erotic wishes develop out of emotional relations of a friendly character, based upon appreciation and admiration (compare Molière's "Kiss me for the love of Greek"[2]), between a master

---

1 Hostile feelings are doubtless a little more complicated in their construction. [In the 1st edition only, this footnote ran: "Hostile feelings, which are a little more complicated in their construction, offer no exception to this rule."]

2 [Quoi! monsieur sait du grec! Ah! permettez, de grâce,
   Que, pour l'amour du grec, monsieur, on vous embrasse.
   *Les femmes savantes*, III, 5.]

and a pupil, between a performer and a delighted listener, and especially in the case of women. In fact the growth of emotional ties of this kind, with their purposeless beginnings, provides a much frequented pathway to sexual object-choice. Pfister, in his *Frömmigkeit des Grafen von Zinzendorf* (1910), has given an extremely clear and certainly not an isolated example of how easily even an intense religious tie can revert to ardent sexual excitement. On the other hand it is also very usual for directly sexual impulsions, short-lived in themselves, to be transformed into a lasting and purely affectionate tie; and the consolidation of a passionate love marriage rests to a large extent upon this process.

We shall naturally not be surprised to hear that the sexual impulsions that are inhibited in their aims arise out of the directly sexual ones when internal or external obstacles make the sexual aims unattainable. The repression during the period of latency is an internal obstacle of this kind—or rather one which has become internal. We have assumed that the father of the primal horde owing to his sexual intolerance compelled all his sons to be abstinent, and thus forced them into ties that were inhibited in their aims, while he reserved for himself freedom of sexual enjoyment and in this way remained without ties. All the ties upon which a group depends are of the character of instincts that are inhibited in their aims. But here we have approached the discussion of a new subject, which deals with the relation between directly sexual instincts and the formation of groups.

D. The last two remarks will have prepared us for finding that directly sexual impulsions are unfavorable to the formation of groups. In the history of the development of the family there have also, it is true, been group relations of sexual love (group marriages); but the more important sexual love became for the ego, and the more it developed the characteristics of being in love, the more urgently it required to be limited to two people—*una cum uno*—as is prescribed by the nature of the genital aim. Polygamous inclinations had to be content to find satisfaction in a succession of changing objects.

Two people coming together for the purpose of sexual satisfaction, in so far as they seek for solitude, are making a demonstration against the herd instinct, the group feeling. The more they are in love, the more completely they suffice for each other. Their rejection of the group's influence is expressed in the shape of a sense of shame. Feelings of jealousy of the most extreme violence are summoned up in order to protect the choice of a sexual object from being encroached upon by a group tie. It is only when the affectionate, that is, personal, factor of a love relation gives place entirely to the sensual one, that it is possible for two people to have sexual intercourse in the presence of others or for there to be simultaneous sexual acts in a group, as occurs at an orgy. But at that point a regression has taken place to an early stage in sexual relations, at which being in love as yet played no part, and all sexual objects were judged to be of equal value, somewhat in the sense of Bernard Shaw's malicious aphorism to the effect that being in love means greatly exaggerating the difference between one woman and another.

There are abundant indications that being in love only made its appearance late on in the sexual relations between men and women; so that the opposition between sexual love and group ties is also a late development. Now it may seem as though this assumption were incompatible with our myth of the primal family. For it was after all by their love for their mothers and sisters that the mob of brothers was, as we have supposed, driven to parricide; and it is difficult to imagine this love as being anything but undivided and primitive—that is, as an intimate union of the affectionate and sensual. But further consideration resolves this objection to our theory into a confirmation of it. One of the reactions to the parricide was after all the institution of totemic exogamy, the prohibition of any sexual relation with those women of the family who had been tenderly loved since childhood. In this way a wedge was driven in between a man's affectionate and sensual feelings, one still firmly fixed in his erotic life today.[1] As a result of this exogamy the sensual needs of men had to be satisfied with strange and unloved women.

In the great artificial groups, the Church and the army, there is no room for woman as a sexual object. The love relation between men and women remains outside these organizations. Even where groups are formed which are composed of both men and women the distinction between the sexes plays no part. There is scarcely any sense in asking whether the libido which keeps groups together is of a homosexual or of a heterosexual nature, for it is not differentiated according to the sexes, and particularly shows a complete disregard for the aims of the genital organization of the libido.

Even in a person who has in other respects become absorbed in a group, the directly sexual impulsions preserve a little of his individual activity. If they become too strong they disintegrate every group formation. The Catholic Church had the best of motives for recommending its followers to remain unmarried and for imposing celibacy upon its priests; but falling in love has often driven even priests to leave the Church. In the same way love for women breaks through the group ties of race, of national divisions, and of the social class system, and it thus produces important effects as a factor in civilization. It seems

[1] See Freud (1912).

certain that homosexual love is far more compatible with group ties, even when it takes the shape of uninhibited sexual impulsions—a remarkable fact, the explanation of which might carry us far.

The psychoanalytic investigation of the psychoneuroses has taught us that their symptoms are to be traced back to directly sexual impulsions which are repressed but still remain active. We can complete this formula by adding—"or, to aim-inhibited impulsions, whose inhibition has not been entirely successful or has made room for a return to the repressed sexual aim." It is in accordance with this that a neurosis should make its victim asocial and should remove him from the usual group formations. It may be said that a neurosis has the same disintegrating effect upon a group as being in love. On the other hand it appears that where a powerful impetus has been given to group formation neuroses may diminish and at all events temporarily disappear. Justifiable attempts have also been made to turn this antagonism between neuroses and group formation to therapeutic account. Even those who do not regret the disappearance of religious illusions from the civilized world of today will admit that so long as they were in force they offered those who were bound by them the most powerful protection against the danger of neurosis.[1] Nor is it hard to discern that all the ties that bind people to mysticoreligious or philosophic-religious sects and communities are expressions of crooked cures of all kinds of neuroses. All of this is correlated with the contrast between directly sexual impulsions and those which are inhibited in their aims.

If he is left to himself, a neurotic is obliged to replace by his own symptom formations the great group formations from which he is excluded. He creates his own world of imagination for himself, his own re-

---

[1] [Cf. the beginning of Section 2 of Freud, 1910.]

ligion, his own system of delusions, and thus recapitulates the institutions of humanity in a distorted way which is clear evidence of the dominating part played by the directly sexual impulsions.[1]

E. In conclusion, we will add a comparative estimate, from the standpoint of the libido theory, of the states with which we have been concerned, of being in love, of hypnosis, of group formation, and of neurosis.

*Being in love* is based on the simultaneous presence of directly sexual impulsions and of sexual impulsions that are inhibited in their aims, while the object draws a part of the subject's narcissistic ego-libido to itself. It is a condition in which there is only room for the ego and the object.

*Hypnosis* resembles being in love in being limited to these two persons, but it is based entirely on sexual impulsions that are inhibited in their aims and puts the object in the place of the ego ideal.

*The group* multiplies this process; it agrees with hypnosis in the nature of the instincts which hold it together, and in the replacement of the ego ideal by the object; but to this it adds identification with other individuals, which was perhaps originally made possible by their having the same relation to the object.

Both states, hypnosis and group formation, are an inherited deposit from the phylogenesis of the human libido—hypnosis in the form of a predisposition, and the group, besides this, as a direct survival. The replacement of the directly sexual impulsions by those that are inhibited in their arms promotes in both states a separation between the ego and the ego ideal, a separation with which a beginning has already been made in the state of being in love.

*Neurosis* stands outside this series. It also is based upon a peculiarity in the development of the human

[1] See *Totem and Taboo*, toward the end of the second essay [*Standard Ed.*, 13, 73–4].

libido—the twice repeated start made by the directly
sexual function, with an intervening period of latency.[1]
To this extent it resembles hypnosis and group formation in having the character of a regression, which is
absent from being in love. It makes its appearance
wherever the advance from directly sexual instincts
to those that are inhibited in their aims has not been
wholly successful; and it represents a *conflict* between
those portions of the instincts which have been re-
ceived into the ego after having passed through this
development and those portions of them which, spring-
ing from the repressed unconscious, strive—as do
other, completely repressed, instinctual impulses—to
attain direct satisfaction. Neuroses are extraordinarily
rich in content, for they embrace all possible relations
between the ego and the object—both those in which
the object is retained and others in which it is aban-
doned or erected inside the ego itself—and also the
conflicting relations between the ego and its ego ideal.

[1] See my *Three Essays* (1905), *Standard Ed.*, 7, 234.

# BIBLIOGRAPHY

Titles of books and periodicals are in italics; titles of papers are in inverted commas. Abbreviations are in accordance with the *World List of Scientific Periodicals* (London, 1952).

Further abbreviations are as follows: *C. P.* = Freud, *Collected Papers* (5 vols.) London, 1924-50. *Standard Ed.* = *Standard Edition* (24 vols.) London, from 1953.

Numerals in thick type refer to volumes; ordinary numerals refer to pages.

For non-technical authors, and for technical authors where no specific work is mentioned, see the Index.

ABRAHAM, K. (1912) "Notes on the Psycho-Analytic Investigation and Treatment of Manic-Depressive Insanity and Allied Conditions," *Selected Papers on Psycho-Analysis,* London, 1927, Chap. VI.

— (1916) "The First Pregenital Stage of the Libido," *Selected Papers on Psycho-Analysis,* London, 1927, Chap. XII.

BLEULER, E. (1912) "Das autistische Denken," *Jb. psychoanal. psychopath. Forsch.*, **4**, 1.

BRUGEILLES, R. (1913) "L'essence du phénomène social: la suggestion," *Rev. phil.*, **75**, 593.

FEDERN, P. (1919) *Die vaterlose Gesellschaft,* Vienna.

FELSZEGHY, BÉLA VON (1920) "Pan und Pankomplex," *Imago,* **6**, 1.

FERENCZI, S. (1909) "Introjection and Transference," *First Contributions to Psycho-Analysis,* London, 1952, Chap. II.

FREUD, S. (1888-9) Preface to Bernheim's *Die Suggestion und ihre Heilwirkung*, C. P. 5, 11; *Standard Ed.*, 1.

— (1895) with BREUER, J., *Studies on Hysteria, Standard Ed.*, 2. (Including Breuer's contributions.)

— (1900) *The Interpretation of Dreams*, London and New York, 1955; *Standard Ed.*, 4-5.

— (1905) "Psychical (or Mental) Treatment," *Standard Ed.*, 7, 283.

— (1905) *Jokes and their Relation to the Unconscious, Standard Ed.*, 8.

— (1905) *Three Essays on the Theory of Sexuality*, London, 1949; *Standard Ed.*, 7, 125.

— (1905) "Fragment of an Analysis of a Case of Hysteria," C. P., 3, 13; *Standard Ed.*, 7, 3.

— (1909) "Analysis of a Phobia in a Five-Year-Old Boy," C. P., 3, 149; *Standard Ed.*, 10, 3.

— (1910) *Leonardo da Vinci and a Memory of his Childhood*, Standard Ed., 11.

— (1910) "The Future Prospects of Psycho-Analytic Therapy," C. P., 2, 285; *Standard Ed.*, 11.

— (1912) "On the Universal Tendency to Debasement in the Sphere of Love," C. P., 4, 203; *Standard Ed.*, 11.

— (1912-13) *Totem and Taboo*, London, 1950; New York, 1952; *Standard Ed.*, 13, 1.

— (1914) "On Narcissism: an Introduction," C. P., 4, 30; *Standard Ed.*, 14.

— (1917) "A Metapsychological Supplement to the Theory of Dreams," C. P., 4, 137; *Standard Ed.*, 14.

— (1917) "Mourning and Melancholia," C. P., 4, 152; *Standard Ed.*, 14.

— (1918) "The Taboo of Virginity," C. P., 4, 217; *Standard Ed.*, 11.

— (1919) "The Uncanny," C. P., 4, 368; *Standard Ed.*, 17.

— (1920) *Beyond the Pleasure Principle*, London, 1950; *Standard Ed.*, 18, 7; Bantam Classics Ed., FC49.

— (1923) *The Ego and the Id*, London, 1927; *Standard Ed.*, 19.

— (1923) "Remarks on the Theory and Practice of Dream-Interpretation," C. P., 5, 136; *Standard Ed.*, 19.

— (1926) *Inhibitions, Symptoms and Anxiety*, London, 1936 (*The Problem of Anxiety*, New York, 1936); *Standard Ed.*, 20.

(1930) *Civilization and its Discontents,* London and New York, 1930; *Standard Ed.,* 21.

(1950) *The Origins of Psycho-Analysis,* London and New York, 1954. (Partly, including "A Project for a Scientific Psychology," in *Standard Ed.,* 1.)

LE BON, G. (1895) *Psychologie des foules,* Paris.

(Trans.: *The Crowd: A Study of the Popular Mind,* London, 1920.)

McDOUGALL, W. (1920) *The Group Mind,* Cambridge.

(1920) "A Note on Suggestion," *J. Neurol. Psychopath.,* 1, 1.

MARCUSZEWICZ, R. (1920) "Beitrag zum autistischen Denken bei Kindern," *Int. Z. Psychoanal.,* 6, 249.

MOEDE, W. (1915) "Die Massen- und Sozialpsychologie im kritischen Überblick," *Z. pädag. Psychol.* 16, 385.

NACHMANSOHN, M. (1915) "Freuds Libidotheorie verglichen mit der Eroslehre Platos," *Int. Z. Psychoanal.,* 3, 65.

PFISTER, O. (1910) *Die Frömmigkeit des Grafen Ludwig von Zinzendorf,* Vienna.

(1921) "Plato als Vorläufer der Psychoanalyse," *Int. Z. Psychoanal.,* 7, 264.

RANK, O. (1922) "Die Don Juan-Gestalt," *Imago,* 8, 142.

RICKMAN, J. (ed.) (1937) *A General Selection from the Works of Sigmund Freud,* London.

SACHS, H. (1920) "Gemeinsame Tagträume," *Int. Z. Psychoanal.,* 6, 395.

SIMMEL, E. (1918) *Kriegsneurosen und "Psychisches Trauma,"* Munich.

SMITH, W. ROBERTSON (1885) *Kinship and Marriage,* London.

TARDE, G. (1890) *Les lois de l'imitation,* Paris.

TROTTER, W. (1916) *Instincts of the Herd in Peace and War,* London.

# INDEX

*Abraham*, 83
Affectivity. *See under* Emotion.
Altruism, 44
Ambivalence, 15, 42, 47
Anaclitic type, 46
Archaic inheritance, 10, 75
Army, 32-36, 67, 72, 85, 94
Autistic mental acts, 4

*Bernheim*, 27, 76
*Bleuler*, 4
Brothers, 33, 88
  in Christ, 33
  community of, 69, 87, 93
*Brugeilles*, 27

*Caesar*, 34
Cathexis, 15, 17, 90
  object-, 44, 46, 54, 58
Catholic Church, 33, 86, 94
Celibacy of priests, 94
Censorship of dreams, 13, 52
Chieftains, Mana in, 73
Children, 13, 14, 15-16, 24, 51,
    62, 70
  fear in, 64, 65-66
  parents and, 42, 65, 89
  sexual object of, 54, 89
  unconscious of, 15
*Christ*, 33-35, 38, 86
  equal love of, 38
  identification with, 86
Church, 32-34, 67-68, 72, 85-86,
    94
Commander-in-Chief, 33-35
Conflict, 15, 82, 97
Conscience, 9, 23, 52, 57, 60
  social, 67
Contagion, emotional, 10-12,
    22, 27, 36

Crowd, 3, 4, 21, 70

Danger, effect on groups, 36-38
*Darwin*, 69
Delusions:
  of inferiority, 82
  of observation, 52
Devotion to abstract idea, 15,
    57
Doubt:
  absence in groups, 13
  interpretation in dreams, 13-
    14
Dream, 17, 52, 80
  interpretation of doubt and
    uncertainty in, 13-14
  symbolism, 88
Duty, sense of, 64, 67, 73

Ego, 10, 15-16, 47-53, 56, 64, 71,
    78-84, 93, 96-97
  relations between ego ideal
    and, 52-53, 79, 81-85
  relations between object and,
    47-53, 56-58, 83-85
Ego ideal, 52, 56-58, 61, 76-79,
    87, 96-97
  abrogation of the, 81
  hypnotist in the place of, 58
  object as substitute for, 56-
    58, 61, 79, 85
  relations between ego and,
    52-53, 79, 81-85
  testing reality of things, 58-59
  the first, 87
Egoism, 44
Emotion:
  ambivalent, 15, 42
  charge of, 22
  contagion of. *See* Contagion

103

Emotion *(continued):*
  intensification of, in groups, 14, 19, 22-24, 26, 36, 62
  primitive induction of, 22, 27, 36
  tender, 55, 60, 89-90
Emotional tie, 31, 33, 35, 40-41, 45, 48, 62, 67, 70, 72, 76, 90-92
  cessation of, 36-38
Empathy, relation to identification, 50, 53
Enthusiasm, in groups, 20
Envy, 66-67
Equality, demand for, 67
Eros, 30-31
Esprit de corps, origin of, 67
Ethical:
  conduct of a group, 15
  level of Christianity, 86
  standards of individual, 20-21

Fairy tales, the hero in, 88
Family, 53, 73, 76, 87, 92
  a group formation, 73
  and Christian community, 33
  and social instinct, 5
  primal, 93
Fascination, 11, 12, 17, 57
Father, 33, 71, 75-76
  equal love of, 72
  God, 89
  identification with, 46-47
  object tie with, 47
  Primal, 71-73, 76, 86-87, 88, 92. deification of, 71, 89. killing the, 72, 87, 93-94
  substitute, 33, 88
Fear:
  children's, 64-65
  in a group, 36-37, 38
  in an individual, 36
  neurotic, 37
  of society, 9
  panic, 35-38
*Federn, P.,* 39

*Felszeghy, Bela von,* 37
*Ferenczi,* 57, 75
Festivals, 81
Folk-lore, 20
Folk-song, 20
French Revolution, 21
Function:
  for testing reality, 17, 58-59

*Gemeingeist,* origin of, 67
Genital organisation, 16
God, 65, 73
  Father, 89
Gregariousness, 63-64, 70
Group:
  artificial, 32-40, 62, 67, 72, 85, 94
  different kinds of, 21, 32
  disintegration of, 37-39
  equality in, 67-68
  fear in, 36
  feeling, 66, 93
  heightened affectivity in. *See under* Emotion.
  ideal, 76, 78
  intellectual capacity of, 12, 15, 19, 20, 23, 24, 26, 62
  intensification of emotion in. *See under* Emotion.
  leaders of. *See under* Leader.
  libidinal structure of, 29, 31, 34-35, 36, 39, 41, 53, 60, 79
  marriages, 92
  mental change of the individual in, 7-12, 26-27, 35, 43, 62, 78
  mind, 4, 6-21, 31, 37, 63
  organisation in, 21, 24-25, 26, 32-33, 60, 62, 69
  primitive, 25, 26, 32, 61
  psychological character of, 7-25
  psychology, 3-5, 7, 20-21, 26-27, 29, 35, 41, 45, 71-72, 78, 86, 88
  revolutionary, 21

Group (continued):
  sexual instincts and, 92
  spirit, 67
  stable, 21, 32, 64, 78
  suggestibility of, 10, 12, 27, 64-65
  transient, 21, 32, 64, 78
Guilt, sense of, 17, 48, 49, 64, 81
Gynaecocracy, 87

Hatred, 41, 43
Hebbel, 37
Herd, 63-65, 68
  instinct, 4, 63-66, 81
Hero, 14, 87-89
Homosexuality, 44, 50-51, 72, 94
Horde Primal, 69-73, 76, 87-88, 92
  father of the. See under Father.
Hypnosis, 10-12, 17, 58-60, 62, 73-76, 96-97
  a group of two, 59, 76
  and sleep, 60, 75
  of fright, 60
Hypnotist, 12, 58, 73-76
Hysteria, identification in, 48-49

Idealisation, 56
Identification, 45-53, 57-58, 64, 66-68, 72, 78-79, 86, 96
  ambivalent, 47
  in hysterical symptom, 48-49
  regression of object-choice to, 48
  with a lost or rejected object, 51, 83-84
  with Christ, 86
  with the father, 46-47
  with the hero, 88
  with the leader, 85
Imitation, 27, 49, 53
Individual:
  a member of many groups, 78
  fear in, 36-37
  mental change in a group, 6-12, 26-27, 35, 43, 62, 78
  psychology, 3-4, 71, 86, 88
Induction of emotion, 22, 27, 36
Infection, mental, 49
Inferiority, delusions of, 81-82
Inheritance, archaic, 10, 75
Inhibition:
  collective, of intellectual functioning, 19, 26
  removal of, 15, 23, 26
Instinct:
  herd, 4, 63-65, 81, 93
  inhibited in aim, 55, 59, 89-97
  life and death, 43
  love, 29, 30, 44
  nutrition, 65
  primary, 64-65
  self-preservative, 26, 65
  sexual, 16, 30, 43, 54-59, 65, 72, 89-96
  social, 4
  inhibited in aim, 55, 59, 72, 89-96
  unconscious, 9
Intellectual ability, lowering of, in groups, 12, 15, 19, 20, 23, 24-25, 26, 62
Introjection, of object into ego, 49, 51, 57

Jealousy, 93

Kings, Mana in, 73
Kraškovič, B. Jnr., 19
Kroeger, 69

Language, 20, 29, 54
Latency, period of, 90, 92, 97
Leader, 17-18, 32, 34-35, 59, 63, 65, 67, 71, 76, 85
  abstractions as substitutes for, 40

Leader *(continued):*
  equal love of, 71, 72
  identification with, 85-86
  killing the, 69
  loss of, 38
  negative, 41
  prestige of, 17-18
  the group ideal, 76, 78, 85
  tie with, 38, 40, 50
*Le Bon,* 6-21, 23, 27, 62, 64, 76, 78
Libidinal:
  structure of the group, 29, 31, 35, 36, 41, 53, 60, 79
  ties, 35, 43-44, 49, 71, 76
  in the group, 35, 39, 41
Libido, 26-31, 34-35, 43, 60, 63, 79, 86, 89, 91, 94, 96
  narcissistic, 44, 56, 71, 80, 96
  oral phase of, 47
  theory, 43, 63, 96
  unification of, 16
  withdrawal of, 83
Love, 29-31, 33, 55, 66, 83, 93-94
  a factor of civilisation, 44, 71
  and character formation, 72, 91-92
  and hatred, 43
  being in, 44, 54-60, 93, 95-97
  child's, 89-90
  Christ's, 33
  equal, 33, 38, 67, 71
  Pauline, 91
  self-. *See under* Narcissism.
  sensual, 54-55, 60, 90
  sexual, 29, 44, 92-94
  sublimated homosexual, 44
  the word, 29-30, 54
  unhappy, 57
  unsensual, 55

*McDougall,* 3, 21-25, 27-28, 36, 37, 64
Magical power of words, 16
Magnetic influence, 10
Magnetism, animal, 73

Mana, 73
Mania, 82-84
*Marcuszewicz,* 51
Marriage, 41, 92
Melancholia, 51, 82-84
Metapsychology, 47, 91
*Moede, Walter,* 19
*Molière,* 91
Morality, totemism the origin of, 69
Mother deities, 87, 89
Multicellularity, 7, 25, 63
Myth, 87-89

*Nachmansohn,* 30
Names, taboo upon, 16
*Napoleon,* 34
Narcissism, 4, 29, 42-44, 52, 56-57, 71, 72, 80
*Nestroy,* 37
Neurosis, 15, 17, 29, 34, 44, 48, 79-80, 95-97
*Nietzsche,* 71
Nutrition, instinct of, 64

Object, 44, 47, 51, 56, 66, 71, 80, 96, 97
  cathexis, 45, 46, 54, 58
  change of, 15, 91, 93
  child's, 54
  –choice, 42, 47, 48, 56, 86, 92, 93
  eating the, 47
  hyper-cathexis of, 58
  identification with ego, 83
  loss or renunciation of, 51, 83
  –love, 43, 48, 56, 86
  relations with the ego, 49, 50-51, 53, 58
  sexual, 50, 54-55, 89
  substituted for ego ideal, 56, 61, 79, 96
Observation, delusions of, 52
Oedipus complex, 46-47, 48, 50, 90
  inverted, 47

Oral phase of organisation of the libido, 47

Organisation in groups, 21, 24-25, 26, 32-33, 60, 62, 69

Orgy, 93

Panic, 35-38

Pan-sexualism, 30

*Paul, Saint*, 30, 91

*Pfister*, 30, 92

*Plato*, 30

Poet, the first epic, 87-88

Power, 9, 13, 22
  of leaders, 17
  of words, 16

Prestige, 17-18, 27

Primitive peoples, 12, 15-16, 19, 70, 73, 81

Psychoanalysis, 5, 8, 13, 15, 28, 30, 45, 46, 64, 75

Psychology:
  group, 3-5, 6, 20-21, 26-27, 29, 35, 41, 45, 70, 72, 78
  group and individual, 3-4, 71, 86, 88

Psychoses, 50, 79

Puberty, 50, 55

Races, repugnance between related, 42

*Rank, Otto*, 86, 88

Rapport, 74

Reality:
  function for testing, 17, 58-59
  contrast between objective and psychological, 17

Regression, 62, 70, 90, 93, 97

Religion, 39, 69
  wars of, 39

Repressed:
  sexual tendencies, 56, 90, 95
  the, 10, 80, 90, 97

Repression, 9, 42, 49, 52, 55, 64, 73, 80, 90, 92

Resistance, 64, 80

Responsibility, sense of, 9, 23-24

*Richter, Konrad*, 28

*Sachs, Hanns*, 14, 88

*Schopenhauer*, 41

Self-:
  consciousness, 23-25
  depreciation, 82
  love. *See under* Narcissism.
  observation, 52
  preservation, 13, 26, 64
  sacrifice, 10, 29, 56

Sex, 30

Sexual:
  act, 70, 93
  aims, 44, 55. Diversion of instinct from, 44. Infantile, 55. Obstacles to, 92
  life, 16, 54
  over-estimation, 56
  tendencies, inhibited and uninhibited, 55, 59, 72, 89-90, 96-97
  union, 29

*Shaw, Bernard*, 93

*Sidis, Boris*, 64

*Sighele*, 19, 21

*Simmel, E.*, 34

Sleep, 75, 80
  and hypnosis, 75

*Smith, Robertson*, 53

Social:
  duties, 67, 73
  relations, 3-4, 44

Socialistic tie, 39

Society, 20, 21, 22, 69
  dread of, 9

Sociology. *See under* Group Psychology.

Speech, 64

Sublimated:
  devotion, 15, 57
  homosexual love, 44

Sublimation, 91

Suggestibility, 10, 11, 27, 64-65

Suggestion, 11-12, 15, 23, 27-28, 31, 63, 73, 76, 79
  counter-, 28
  definition for, 76
  mutual, 11, 22, 27, 63
Superman, 71

Taboo, 16, 73, 86
*Tarde*, 27
Totemism, 69, 87
Totemistic:
  clan, 73
  community of brothers, 87
  exogamy, 94
Tradition, 14, 18
  of the group, 24
  of the individual, 25
Transference, 74-75
*Trotter*, 25, 63-65, 68, 81

Uncanniness, 73, 76

Uncertainty, absence in groups, 13-14
  interpretation in dreams, 13-14
Unconscious, 8, 9, 11, 13-14, 15, 19, 48, 51, 55, 74, 76, 80
  groups led by, 13
  instincts, 9
  *Le Bon's*, 9-10, 13, 20
  of children, 15, 90
  of neurotics, 15
  racial, 8

*Wallenstein*, 34
War neuroses, 34
War, the, 34
*Wilson, President*, 35
Wishes, affective cathexis of, 17
Words, magical power of, 16